Althea Copper
Belinda Cordwell
Annabel Croft
Heather Crowe
Isabelle Cueto
Kathleen Cummings
Brigitte Cuypers
Svetlana Cherneva
    Parkhomenko

D

Jose-Luis Damiani
Larry Davidson
Phil Davies
Martin Davis
Marty Davis
Scott Davis
Chris Delaney
Jim Delaney
Horacio De La Pena
Tracy Delatte
Phil Dent
Steve Denton
Mike DePalmer
Manuel Diaz
Eddie Dibbs
Colin Dibley
Brett Dickinson
Mark Dickson
Carlos DiLaura
Jai DiLouie
Steve Docherty
Patrice Dominguez
Gary Donnelly
Peter Doohan
Colin Dowdeswell
David Dowlen
Brad Drewett
Randy Druz
Cliff Drysdale
Robin Drysdale
Lawson Duncan
Ivan Dupasquier
Pat DuPre
Brod Dyke

Jill Davis
Petra Delhees
Isabelle Demongeot
Emmanuelle Derly
Diane Desfor
Ann Devries
Niege Dias
Amanda Dingwall
Cynthia Doerner
Lisa Doherty
Dianne Donnelly
Lilian Drescher

Laura DuPont
Jo Durie
Francoise Durr
Jeanne DuVall

E

John Eagleton
Stefan Edberg
Mark Edmondson
Craig Edwards
Eddie Edwards
Ahmed El Mehelmy
Roy Emerson
Stefan Eriksson
Mike Estep
Kelly Evernden
Rand Evett

Katja Ebbinghaus
Elisabeth Ekblom
Leigh Anne Eldredge
Lynn Epstein
Dianne Evers
Chris Evert
Jeanne Evert

F

Rick Fagel
Charlie Fancutt
Michael Fancutt
John Feaver
Peter Feigl
Ernie Fernandez
Wojtek Fibak
Alvaro Fillol
Jaime Fillol
Mike Fishbach
Rick Fisher
John Fitzgerald
Ken Flach
Peter Fleming
Jean Fleurian
Marc Flur
Guy Forget
Bruce Foxworth
John Frawley
Marcel Freeman
Christophe Freyss
Eric Friedler
Bernard Fritz
Guy Fritz
Harry Fritz
Eric Fromm

Rosalyn Fairbank
Diane Farrell
Jackie Fayter

Karen Feldman
Patty Fendick
Anna-Maria Fernandez
Gigi Fernandez
Maria Fernandez
Mary Joe Fernandez
Louise Field
Julie Filkoff
Shawn Foltz
Jane Forman
Lele Forood
Rayni Fox
Kathy Foxworth
Amy Frazier
Debbie Freeman
Dianne Fromholtz
Bettina Fulco

G

Mike Gandolfo
Tim Garcia
Joe Garcia
Alejandro Ganzabal
Alvin Gardiner
Chris Garner
Alejandro Gattiker
Rolf Gehring
Rejean Genois
John Geraghty
Vitas Gerulaitis
Sammy Giammalva
Tony Giammalva
Brad Gilbert
Hans Gildemeister
Bob Giltinan
Warren Girle
Drew Gitlin
Shlomo Glickstein
Julio Goes
Dan Goldie
Andres Gomez
Francisco Gonzalez
Tom Gorman
Brian Gottfried
Georges Goven
Jim Grabb
Clark Graebner
David Graham
Tony Graham
Jiri Granat
Mike Grant
R
W
M
Tom Gullikson
Jan Gunnerson

Heinz Gunthardt
Marcus Gunthardt
Jimmy Gurfein

Bonnie Gadusek
Gretchen Galt
Donna Ganz
Zina Garrison
Laura Garrone
Linda Gates
Barbara Gerken
Ruta Gerulaitis
Dana Gilbert
Wendy Gilchrist
Raquel Giscafre
Liliane Giussani
Gail Glasgow
Laura Golarsa
Jamie Golder
Sabrina Goles
Sara Gomer
Kate Gompert
Viviana Gonzalez
Jennifer Goodling
Evonne Goolagong
Lucy Gordon
Shannon Gordon
Steffi Graf
Nerida Gregory
Ann Grossman
Michele Gurdal

H

Chico Hagey
Greg Halder
George Hardie
Rodney Harmon
John Hayes
Garth Haynes
Wayne Hearn
Bob Hewitt
Ron Hightower
Jose Higueras
Per Hjertqvist
Jakob Hlasek
Marcos Hocevar
Joel Hoffman
Thomas Hogstedt
Greg Holmes
Charles Honey
Chip Hooper
Jiri Hrebec
Rob Hubbard

Susan Hagey
Sonia Hahn
Elly Hakami
Julie Halard

Barbara Hallquist
Sylvia Hanika
Dee Ann Hansel
Tanya Harford
Julie Harrington
Kathy Harter
Ann Henricksson
Kelly Henry
Jean Hepner
Beth Herr
Nathalie Herreman
Jane Hetherington
Jill Hetherington
Anne Hobbs
Andrea Holikova
Terry Holladay
Amy Holton
Kathy Holton
Kathleen Horvath
Linda Howell
Petra Huber
Karin Huebner
Lesley Hunt
Felicia Hutnick
Patricia Hy

I

Marcelo Ingaramo
Erick Iskersky
Haroon Ismail

Etusko Inoue
Anna Ivan

J

Martin Jaite
John James
Andrew Jarrett
Eric Jelen
Luke Jensen
Kjell Johansson
Jerome Jones
Kelly Jones
Deon Joubert

Andrea Jaeger
Susan Jaeger
Michelle Jaggard
Mima Jausovec
Monique Javer
Debbie Jevans
Catrin Jexell
Penny Johnson
Christiane Jolissaint
Elizabeth Jones
Barbara Jordan
Kathy Jordan

K

Chris Kachel
George Kalovelonis
Jerry Karzen
Chris Kennedy
Steve Kennedy
Kevin Kerns
Carlos Kirmayr
Jeff Klaparda
Bruce Kleege
Ivan Kley
Roger Knapp
Jan Kodes
Andy Kohlberg
Eric Korita
Mark Kratzman
Aaron Krickstein
Johan Kriek
Ramesh Krishnan
Steve Krulevitz
Jan Kukal
Michael Kures

Angeliki Kanellopoulou
Jaime Kaplan
Carina Karlsson
Kathrin Keil
Helen Kelesi
Petra Keppeler
Akiko Kijimuta
Grace Kim
Billie Jean King
Kristin Kinney
Ann Kiyomura-Hayashi
Beatrice Klein
Jenny Klitch
Ilana Kloss
Claudia Kohde-Kilsch
Eva Krapl
Marian Kremer
Marise Kruger
Iwona Kuczynska
Caroline Kuhlman
Kathy Kuykendall

L

Jay Lapidus
Marcelo Lara
Leonardo Lavalle
Rod Laver
Glenn Layendecker
Mike Leach
Rick Leach
Henri Leconte
Cary Leeds
Ivan Lendl
John Leonard

US OPEN

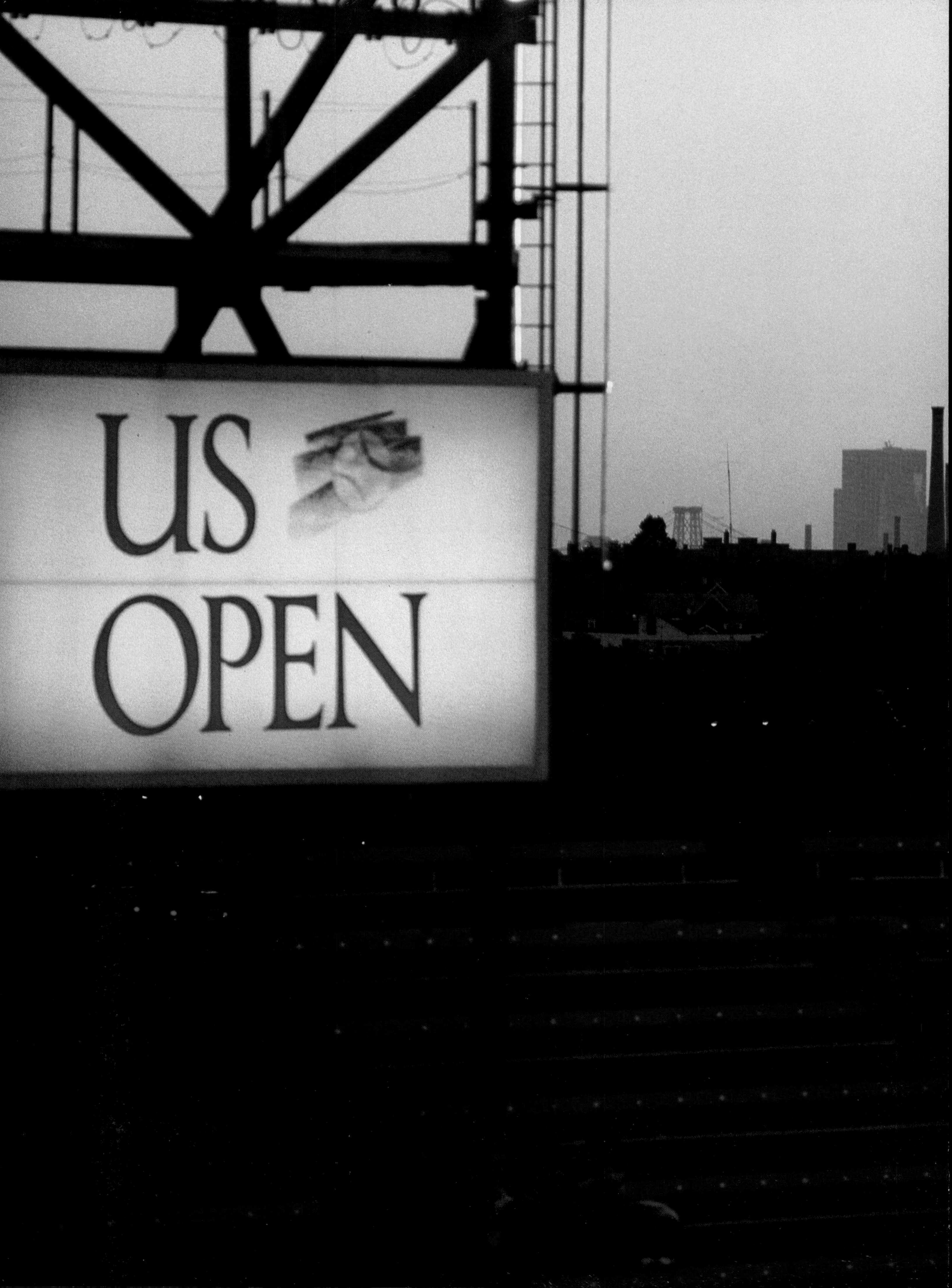
US
OPEN

US OPEN

at the USTA National Tennis Center

Taylor Publishing Company, Dallas, Texas

Written by Moira J. Saucer
with Paul "Pete" Graves, Jr.

Photographs by Russ Adams

Copyright 1988 by United States Tennis Association

All photographs are copyrighted in the name of
Russ Adams.

Additional Photo Credits:
David Walberg, Peter Meyers, Mark Kellam,
Tom Fey, John Mackintosh

Designed by Wondriska Associates, Inc.

Published by Taylor Publishing Company

Library of Congress Cataloging in Publication Data:

Saucer, Moira.
    The U.S. Open at the National Tennis Center/photographs by Russ Adams.
        p.   cm.
    Text by Moira Saucer and Pete Graves.
    ISBN 0-67833-591-9: $19.95
    1. U.S. Open Championships, New York, N.Y.   I. Adams, Russ.
II. Graves, Pete. III. Title.
GV999.S28 1988   88-15922
796.342'09747'1—dc19   CIP

Dedicated to all the players
who have played the
U.S. Open at the
USTA National Tennis Center.

Contents

A C K N O W L E D G E M E N T S

It is virtually impossible to recall the many magazine and newspaper articles read and conversations held with those personally involved in the U.S. Open move to the USTA National Tennis Center. But these have all combined for this first-time telling of an important tennis story.

Thanks are in order to those of the USTA, Mike Burns, Ed Fabricius, Buford L. Driskill, Jr., Bruce Levy, Lesley Poch, JoAnne Fairchild, Suzanne Maguire and general counsel George Gowen; and of course, to Slew Hester, past president of the USTA, whose wisdom, foresight and energy in 1977 were the catalysts in the move to Flushing Meadows.

To Russ Adams, whose photographs appear on the pages of this book and to Janice Gage, assistant to Russ Adams, for the photographic research.

To Moira Saucer who provided the words for the book; Paul "Pete" Graves, Jr. whose countless hours of research and early drafts of portions of the manuscript gave us a puzzle's outline. Thanks to Paddi Valentine for her research and help with photo captions. A gracious thanks to Dr. Ann Woodlief, who provided editorial assistance. This past decade of the U.S. Open will always be noted for its influence on the game. Here is the story from the thoughts of those involved.

Don J. Beville

The U.S. Open Tennis Championships has become one of the world's premier sporting events, thanks in no small part to the creation of the USTA National Tennis Center in Flushing Meadows.

The Open in New York has added a colorful and democratic tint to this most international sport. Each year, young men and women from all over the world come here for two exciting weeks bringing their skill and optimism to us. The city and citizens of New York have responded with growing enthusiasm. In ten short years, the U.S. Open has taken on the flavor of New York; and New Yorkers have become among the keenest and most knowledgeable of tennis fans. Whether playing on the courts 50 weeks in the year or watching from the stands at the end of each summer, New Yorkers are grateful to their city and to the USTA for building the National Tennis Center here.

All of us who have enjoyed the championships wish the U.S. Open continuing success. Congratulations to the champions of the past and to the winners of the 1988 U.S. Open.

Henry A. Kissinger

USTA National Tennis Center
SITE OF THE U.S. OPEN TENNIS CHAMPIONSHIPS

LEFT: The 1881 men's singles championship pin awarded to R. D. Sears, the first U.S. National Champion.

BELOW: Tom Okker (left) and Arthur Ashe following the 1968 U.S. Open finals.

CHAPTER **1** *The Spirit of the Open*

In 1968, the U.S. Open made its grand debut, with the first "pro-am" match at the West Side Tennis Club in Forest Hills, New York. Tennis had exploded as a major American sport, and no one knew it better than the fans. About 30,000 more fans than the previous year came out to watch amateur Arthur Ashe overtake Tom Okker of the Netherlands. Beating Ken Rosewall in the semifinals, Okker won the $14,000 prize for the competing pros.

Well, what in the world was the big *hurrah* all about? It was none other than the advent of "Open Tennis." Since the very early days of lawn tennis, the lines were marked and carefully drawn between amateur and professional tennis. The amateur took trophies and money for expenses only, although stories persist about under-the-table payments. The amateur player who joined the world of the professional player signed on for a lonely life, barred from amateur events such as the U.S. Nationals.

The professionals got too good to ignore, finally, and between 1967 and 1968, debate over competition between professionals and amateurs got steamy. The United States Lawn Tennis Association (USLTA), an early advocate of open tennis, saw it come to fruition in 1968, when this new open category allowed pro players to enter the formerly amateur tournaments and compete for prize money. The unique new open tennis brought the pros back into the mainstream of competitive tennis and out of the local gyms where they played on their exhibition match tours.

In tournaments to come, record numbers of fans packed the stands, amazed by the feats of Chris Evert, Billie Jean King, Jimmy Connors, Ilie Nastase, John McEnroe, Bjorn Borg, Ivan Lendl, and Martina Navratilova at the U.S. Open. American tennis had become great tennis and needed a major new tournament home. *Voila!* Slew Hester waved his magic wand and . . . the move to Flushing Meadows. Expanding crowds have pushed the 1978 U.S. Open attendance of 275,300 to a record-breaking paid attendance of 413,821 in 1986.

Televised coverage took the tennis revolution and the U.S. Open to the fans back home. Before 1968, they could rely on partial coverage from the final two days of the Forest Hills championship. By 1987, daily coverage by network and cable television enabled the U.S. Open to reach many millions who could not attend.

The U.S. Open has become the top prize money tournament in the world, with a 1987 purse of $3,979,294, the highest ever. Although the prize money and the tough competition of the U.S. Open have made it seem too commercial to some, true tennis fans and the players both know

16

that the U.S. Open is a test of stamina, determination, and skill. Some consider it the toughest tennis competition in the world. The U.S. Open's pull is as strong as ever to athletes everywhere.

Since the first U.S. Open at Flushing Meadows, the New York atmosphere, the fans, and the facility have been sources of passionate discussion for the press and the United States Tennis Association (USTA). So much so, that adding up the points for and against any given Open has become as much a ritual as the tournament itself. The outspoken New York fans, the planes flying overhead from LaGuardia, and the demanding surface make Flushing Meadows a most unique place to hit a ball. Want a strawberries and cream atmosphere? Flushing Meadows is not the place. How about night life, crowds that participate, and the heady contrast between exhilaration and tension of the final Grand Slam of the year?

The USTA made its own major commitment to Flushing Meadows a few years back, but that's for the next chapter. Suffice it to say that the USTA has made yearly changes to make the tournament a better place for the fans who flood the gates each August. The International Food Village, completed in 1982, brings the ethnic mood of New York right where it belongs—to the heart of an event as democratic and American as Mom, apple pie, and a Coney Island hot dog. The new message boards with up-to-date information on matches, the replacement of backless seats with those with backs, and considerable landscaping are all moves to make the fans feel more comfortable. For the players six new practice courts have made preparing for matches easier.

The game of tennis in the United States owes a debt to the U.S. Open. Each year, the United States Tennis Association passes on greater revenues to tennis organizations throughout the country. The USTA, which runs the U.S. Open, as the nation's oldest amateur sports governing body, takes its role seriously in developing tennis on all levels, from the grassroots to the pros. Tennis will keep growing, too, through the national programs and those offered by the association's 17 sections. Mainly through the USTA, but also through recreation departments, tennis industry organizations, teaching pros, and scholastic and collegiate coaches, tennis has become a national sport.

A USTA official put it better than anyone else, when he said, "In terms of assets, the USTA is not measured so much in typewriters, desks, computers, bricks, and mortar as much as in people and their attitudes. That is the essence of the U.S. Open. It represents the spirit of tennis in the United States. It is truly the 'crown jewel' of the USTA."

". . . people and their attitudes. That is the essence of the US Open."

An aerial view of the ash dump
before the transformation for the
1939–40 New York World's Fair.

CHAPTER 2 "Give Them Beauty for Ashes"

"This facility represents the best in cooperation between the public and private sectors; as well as the evolution of tennis from the country club to the public park, from a sport for the privileged few to a game of the masses."

New York Mayor Ed Koch, at the finals
of the 1978 U.S. Open Tennis Championships

Those listening to Mayor Koch's words surely recognized the beginning of a new era for U.S. tennis. Almost by a sleight of hand, the fans stood in the stadium of New York's previously decaying Louis Armstrong stadium, now brilliantly refurbished. It would be open not only to the stars of the U.S. Open tournament, but also for the other heroes—the ordinary players—who could rent public court time and have their chance to chase balls in the dusty footprints of their favorite players.

Few may have fully understood that the USTA National Tennis Center's inception resulted largely from the foresight of one man—W.E. (Slew) Hester, then USTA president. Described by the press as *determined*, Hester, in a far-reaching motion to shift the tournament from Forest Hills to Flushing Meadows, would provide fans and the public with an accessible focus for a sport dramatically increasing in popularity. Hester had early recognized tennis as an important national trend which would become a game for all and a growing obsession for a new generation of younger players and their fans.

Hester had the business sense to carry through with his plans to establish and maintain better facilities for the tournament that had outgrown its home at Forest Hills. Since 1972, he had been an independent oil producer. His previous experience included many incarnations—sales manager, then executive vice-president, first of a trucking and air-conditioning distributorship and then an oil company. Earlier, he had received his World War II assignment in Northern Europe with the noted Red Ball Express, the military's transportation outfit. Over the years Hester had also made a name for himself as a fine tennis player as well as an active participant and administrator for numerous tennis organizations.

During the year before the opening of the National Tennis Center, magazines and newspapers had detailed the reasons that the USTA wished to move the tournament from Forest Hills to Flushing Meadows. Hester himself had written to the Executive Committee of the USTA that the or-

U.S. Open officials Slew Hester,
Joseph Carrico and ITF President
Philippe Chatrier (left to right)
plant ivy at the opening ceremonies
of the USTA National Tennis Center.

ganization and the West Side Tennis Club's arrangement had been "mutually beneficial over a period of more than 50 years." In his own succinct fashion, Hester had noted, "The location at Forest Hills has been attractive for many reasons, and the Club has provided a traditional atmosphere which many find appealing. It is, however, unpopular with the players because of its cramped and somewhat limited facilities. The lack of parking is a drawback, and substantial capital improvements are long overdue."

Economic considerations also figured heavily in the USTA's decision to move the tournament. In October 1976, Hester had presented Lindley Hoffman, the president of the West Side Tennis Club, with a proposal to finance certain improvements in the Club, but disagreements between the USTA and the private West Side Tennis Club could not be resolved. The West Side Tennis Club had suggested a plan to renovate the club house, build new locker rooms, a new indoor tennis facility, renovate and enlarge the stadium and other improvements and amenities. The U.S. Open Championships would cover these costs, estimated to be from $5,000,000 – $7,000,000.

Hester remembers the last meeting between the USTA and the West Side Tennis Club in January 1977:

> *Joe Carrico, Marvin Richmond, Mike Burns, and George Gowen represented the USTA; members of the West Side Board of Directors and officers represented West Side. There was a pleasant dinner meeting. After dinner, when the discussion of the contract began, the speaker for West Side said, 'Our members want the improvements and facilities we have requested, or we don't want the tournament.' A quick poll of the USTA representatives indicated a firm refusal. I said to Mike Burns, 'Mike, sign the dinner check'—and we all departed.*

The USTA had only 19 months in which to make arrangements to hold the U.S. Open elsewhere.

Some protested the move as a blow to tennis tradition in the United States. Forest Hills meant "real tradition," a link to a gracious past. Although the grass courts there had eventually given way to a clay surface, professional competition, and large crowds, the tournaments at Forest Hills still had the feeling of gentility about them. A move would destroy the sense of history for some people and the tradition of tennis played since 1915 against the backdrop of a striped marquee and the Tudor gothic clubhouse.

"If the public reacts to the lack of ivy . . . We will plant ivy."

Hester's response to these critics was as American as his desire to nationalize tennis. He had said, "If the public reacts to the lack of ivy . . . we will plant ivy." And he kept his promise by planting some ivy in a large container on the grounds of the National Tennis Center.

There was a certain appropriate quality to Hester's discovery of the future location for the U.S. Open, for he did seem to have a talent for the Big Picture. He flew into New York in 1977 from Jackson, Mississippi to discuss possible sites for the tournament with New York City Parks Commissioner Martin Lang. As his plane headed into LaGuardia Airport that wintry January day, he gazed beneath him at Flushing Meadows-Corona Park in Queens. Looking at an abandoned stadium framed by the

ABOVE: Attending the ground breaking ceremonies were: Joe Davidson, Commissioner of Parks and Recreation, City of New York; Donald Manes, President, Borough of Queens; Mrs. Louis Armstrong; Slew Hester, president of the USTA; and Alan King (left to right).

OPPOSITE, TOP: Architect David Specter presents the construction plans for the USTA National Tennis Center to the press.

OPPOSITE, BOTTOM: New construction and renovation begin at the USTA National Tennis Center.

snow, Hester suddenly saw embodied in the old Louis Armstrong stadium below him a map for action, a concrete plan.

Hester had previously discussed with New Orleans Mayor Moon Landrieu his dilemma, the problem of finding an alternative home for the U.S. Open. "Moon had been the head of the National Mayors Conference and [had] helped bail New York out of its fiscal problems, so I knew he would put me in touch with the right people," said Hester at the time. The rest is tennis history.

Hester could have hardly chosen a site more representative of American sweat and toil than Flushing Meadows. The park boasted an unlikely history. F. Scott Fitzgerald had bestowed upon the marshy land a questionable immortality in *The Great Gatsby*, characterizing it as a wasteland, a dumping ground for New Yorkers, a bed of ashes viewed by travelers out of Long Island train windows: "This is a valley of ashes—a fantastic farm where ashes grow like wheat into ridges and hills and grotesque gardens," wrote Fitzgerald. A previously rich tidal basin, Flushing Meadows would remain an ash heap, used by the Brooklyn Ash Removal Company, until the 1930s when the Long Island Parks Commission announced plans to clear a portion of Flushing Meadows for the Grand Central Parkway, which would link Triborough Bridge with arterial Queens parkways.

Nearly as large as its sister Central Park, The Flushing Meadows—Corona Park area measured about two-and-a-half miles long and was 1000 feet to a half-mile wide. Filling the deep marshy areas—the mires—and leveling the monumental ash dumps, some in 200 foot mountainous ridges, made the task of clearing Flushing Meadows a project for decades.

Hester already had the determined efforts of an earlier New York Commissioner of Parks—Robert Moses—to thank for the existence of Flushing Meadows as it appears today. When Moses first decided to clear the land in the 1920s, he had in mind eventually turning Flushing Meadows into a recreational park.

Moses had guided the efforts to bring the World's Fairs to Flushing Meadows, encountering monumental difficulties. New construction at the site included two sewage plants to clean up Flushing Bay's pollution, as well as a large drainage system for the Flushing Meadows area in its entirety. But in the war years of the 1940s, Flushing Meadows disintegrated.

Moses managed, however, to garner further monies for the park's improvement when, at his suggestion, the City Building became the temporary United Nations Headquarters in the 1950s. A portion of the allocation for building renovations went to improve the park area. With the 1964-65 Worlds's Fair, Moses continued his efforts to make Flushing Meadows a major city landmark.

Robert Moses believed, as he once wrote, in Emerson's theory that "an institution is the lengthened shadow of one man." He would certainly have had his belief confirmed by Hester's achievement. Hester's transformation of the Louis Armstrong Stadium within a year after announcing the U.S. Open's move to Flushing Meadows would guarantee the USTA's legacy to New York City and assure Flushing Meadows worldwide recognition.

27

The site Hester had chosen had been virtually abandoned by the city after efforts to renovate it further had failed. The Louis Armstrong Stadium had initially been constructed for the 1964-65 World's Fair. Originally named Singer Bowl, it had been renamed The Arena in 1967. Others before Hester had seen promise in the 15,000 seat stadium, including Warner Communications Company, which had advanced a proposal in 1972 to turn the facility into a soccer stadium and to use it for public events, such as musical concerts. As a promotional gesture, Warner had wanted the stadium renamed Warner Bowl and had made its offer contingent on the city granting its request.

In 1972, however, the city renamed The Arena the Louis Armstrong Stadium. On signing the City Council legislation to rename it, Mayor John V. Lindsay said, "It is thoroughly fitting that this cultural and civic center be named after one of our truly great New Yorkers, a man who spent much of his life just a few blocks from the stadium now bearing his name." (Famed jazz musician Louis Armstrong had lived in Corona for more than 38 years).

In the early 1970s, the city had spent $380,000 to renovate the stadium, including the construction of a new stage, seats, and facade. After this promising beginning, however, the city closed the Louis Armstrong Stadium in 1974. The structure did not meet standards for a permanent certificate of occupancy.

Armed with a park department map of the Flushing Meadows-Corona Park area, Hester and USTA Executive Secretary Burns went to take a look at Flushing Meadows the same day Hester flew over the stadium: "The area looked promising, and the stadium looked good. It was under two feet of snow, which gave it a clean and sterile appearance. Since we had a north wind that day, we had no plane noise."

On January 25, 1977, Hester presented New York City officials with plans for a National Tennis Center. At that time, the proposal included a plan to renovate the stadium, at a cost to the USTA of $5,000,000, to construct between 16-32 outdoor courts with lighting, and to build 9 indoor courts with locker room facilities. Financing for the National Tennis Center would be through a construction loan, secured with the USTA's television contract as the main collateral.

The same day that Hester presented his idea to the city, he procured a signed agreement by the Mayor. He says, "the only change was that we had to have a plat of the 16 plus acres, a proposed layout, and this had to be ready for the Board of Estimates the next day." He and Burns had to find an architect quickly. They called Lew Rudin, chairman of the Association for a Better New York. The USTA's Communications Director Ed Fabricius recalls, "To Rudin it [the National Tennis Center] was important." Rudin would be instrumental in setting up meetings with key city officials. With a list of capable architects in hand, Hester and Burns got right on the phone. Only one of the architects—David Kenneth Specter—was in his office at 7:00 p.m. that day. Hester and Burns hailed a cab and went to his office. The next morning Specter had a crew ready, and Hester had his plat for the city.

Soon after, Hester presented the USTA with his plans. He had a sales agenda, a time table, and a budget. Meeting with both the old management committee and a newly-elected one, he received the blessings of both.

The USTA presented the Department of Parks and Recreation with a formal proposal for the project in March. The USTA made clear, at that time, its intention to provide tennis courts to the public for reasonable rental fees. The USTA would be responsible for the maintenance of the courts. It would have 60 days per year for its own events and would co-sponsor other tennis events with New York City. The USTA's proposal to renovate and make capital improvements would extend over a lease term of 12 years.

By then, the USTA was moving rapidly on what Hester refers to as a "fast track construction job." While certain phases of the job were in progress, plans for others were being made. The City of New York Department of Parks and Recreation and the USTA signed a "Memorandum of Understanding" for a 15-year lease term on May 26, 1977.

The USTA agreed to pay all construction, financing, maintenance, and operating costs, in addition to paying the City of New York at least $125,000 a year to use the stadium and property, a figure to be adjusted annually depending on the Consumer Price Index. In addition to earlier agreements already detailed, the USTA also stated, "It is the intention of the USTA to conduct free tennis clinics and tennis programs in cooperation with the city of New York and other recognized civic and community organizations." In August 1977, the USTA and the City of New York signed a Permit Agreement which set the USTA's opening date no later than August 28, 1978.

Comedian Alan King, city and Queens borough officials, and Mrs. Louis Armstrong as well as USTA personnel braved the rain for a groundbreaking ceremony in October 1977. Hester said, "This left us ten months on a job that experienced New Yorkers said would take four years. Sometimes, it's a blessing to be a dumb Southerner." Many still wonder how Hester finished the work on time. The renovations were extensive, while the complexities of the New York City bureaucracy could have made construction deadlines hard to meet. In retrospect, Michael Burns, the executive secretary of the USTA, says:

> I think it's . . . his personality. I think he may have disarmed some of these people [city officials] because he was so frank and open in discussion with them . . . some of them may have thought 'Well, here is a Southern boy from Jackson, Mississippi. What does he want?' But then, when they heard him out, it made sense. It was good for the City . . . The City didn't pay for anything, which I'm sure the City liked. The first [sic] Parks Commissioner, Marty Lang, was from someplace down South, and I remember Slew talked to him about going catfishing down on the Pearl River. Good ole boy stuff. . . .

Despite difficulties and warnings to the contrary, for the most part the construction process proceeded fairly well. The crews unearthed old pilings from World's Fair buildings, many of which had been demolished after the fairs according to the City's building requirements. Builders also discovered a tidal water table under an old landfill of 6-8 feet depth. Through the winter, the workers battled the elements. If that weren't enough, seven unions went on strike in New York City.

It took a lot of persistence to get such an enormous project organized in such a short time, but Hester had a lot of help. Cooperative city officials assisted with the tangle of agencies and formalities. Marty Lang had been instrumental in the early phases of the project. Later, Gordon Davis would become parks commissioner. He and Donald Manes, then Queens' borough president, offered guidance and help. Says Hester: "We were able to secure permits and inspection in reasonable time. The future looked rosy and bright."

The on-site manager for H.R.H. construction, Len Borgida, supervised the fast track construction and worked to avoid delays, in what Hester calls a "masterful job." Hy Zausner offered his help as a "knowledgeable volunteer" to be a "daily watch dog, and on-site expediter," Hester remembers.

Surprises did occur. Hester recalls receiving a phone call from Consolidated Edison after the company had run a survey in May showing the center's power requirements would blow out every transformer and light in the surrounding area. The two alternatives were to dig an underground line for nearly a mile for new service, at a cost of $900,000, or else get two transformers. If they could get the transformers, Consolidated Edison would run power from Long Island Rail, only 100 feet away. Says Hester "These were no ordinary transformers . . . . On inquiry, delivery was 18 months to 2 years . . . . After an anxious phone call, a day's search, we found two transformers in Ruston, Louisiana . . . . We were able to buy them and avert the catastrophe."

"They had installed the transformers, but no one had ordered the power switches. 'What a light bill.' "

When Hester arrived in New York several days before the opening of the National Tennis Center, he found the entire complex ablaze with light in the middle of the night. They had installed the transformers, but no one had ordered power switches. "What a light bill!" he remembers. The lights had been on continuously for 21 days.

The finished complex would give players, fans, and the press the finest modern tennis championship facilities in the world. The Louis Armstrong Stadium had been divided into two stadia—the 20,000 seat main stadium and the 6,000 Grandstand Court. There were now nine air-conditioned indoor courts and 27 outdoor courts. Seating on outside courts made a great number of additional seats available. Finally, the players got their due, with private locker rooms and a lounge. And the fans could sit and eat to their heart's content, with a host of eating areas available. If they got tired of tennis, they could lounge on the grass. There was room for everyone.

And Hester's feelings about the move?

We finished on time—History was made, 10 months to do a job that was estimated at 4 years. Cost? Sure it ran over the initial budget. In fact, I'm not sure we had a budget. We only had time to build, not to worry about plans, costs, and details. Before the National Tennis Center, the USTA operated on some $300,000–$400,000. The Management Committee complained that we authorized club sandwiches for lunch but not strawberry tarts for desserts. Yes, those were the good ole days—I hope they don't come back!

Slew Hester, USTA president, speaking
at the opening ceremonies.

Bob Hewitt (left) and Bjorn Borg
anticipate their first match at
the USTA National Tennis Center.

Former CBS-TV Sports Commentator Jack Whitaker put it all in perspective on the day of the 1978 finals:

> *A few years ago Joe Raposo wrote a wonderful song called, "There Used to Be a Ball Park Right Here." The song recalls as we tear down our old ball parks and put up apartment houses or other things in their places.*
>
> *Well, the place we're sitting today, right here in this tennis center, used to be a dump; and it's now a sporting facility that bids to be one of the finest in the world. Flushing Meadows.*
>
> *Flushing Meadows has been many things in its long and checkered career, and it was no one less than F. Scott Fitzgerald that gave its other life a certain immortality in* The Great Gatsby.
>
> *Flushing Meadows is what he wrote, a certain desolate area, a valley of ashes, where ashes grow like wheat.*
>
> *Well, in the years since Gatsby passed through here on his way to West Egg, the dump has been filled in. It was filled in by a gentleman named Fishhooks McCarthy from Brooklyn; and you might surmise that Fishhooks ran an ash removal company.*
>
> *Robert Moses then made the Meadow into a park. It has been the campus for two World's Fairs, and now is the home of the National Championship of the United States Tennis Association.*
>
> *It is in this last role that Flushing Meadow may get its lasting reputation.*
>
> *This tennis center sits right across the Long Island Railroad tracks from Shea Stadium; and the juxtaposition is almost heroic. You see, Shea Stadium was built with taxpayers' money, and then practically given to one of the richest families in America, which ran it as their very own.*
>
> *This tennis facility sits on land owned by the city. But the construction was paid for by the United States Tennis Association. It's an example of intelligent cooperation between city government and the private sector. That's the first thing in its favor.*
>
> *The second thing in its favor is space and room—space and room for players, space and room for spectators.*
>
> *Yes. It's noisy. The Long Island Railroad does not exactly run on rubber wheels, and the planes coming in and out of LaGuardia on certain days are very low, and very loud. But those are the sounds of the 70s.*
>
> *The place has a certain new look about it, an erector set look about it. But that will change as the trees grow and the ivy climbs.*
>
> *Tradition? They already have it here. The tennis this week has been superb.*
>
> *Flushing Meadows. There used to be a dump right here, but not anymore.*

CHAPTER 3 *1978–1980: The Crown Jewel*

An international array of fans converged to greet players on August 29, 1978 for the opening of the red, white, and blue USTA National Tennis Center. They marked an occasion worth celebrating for tennis fans everywhere—the construction of the first major championship tennis facility since France's *Stade Roland Garros* opened in 1928. "What we are witnessing here, at the former home of two celebrated World's Fairs, is not only one of the most illustrious sporting spectacles in the world, but also the accomplishment of a unique venture," said Slew Hester in his welcoming remarks. "The fact that a national governing body, in any sport, could develop a site such as the one being dedicated at these Championships, is something everyone can be proud of."

The opening match, played at night, which top-seed Bjorn Borg won against Bob Hewitt, 6–0, 6–2, initiated a new era of tennis, an "ultra-Open era" of phenomenal growth for the sport. The United States, Sweden, Czechoslovakia and West Germany produced all the singles finalists and champions in the first ten years of the U.S. Open at the National Tennis Center. In the upcoming years, the USTA would continue to strengthen its community efforts to nurture tennis throughout the United States. Likewise, a number of European countries would provide younger players with help and support necessary to excel in the game.

In the men's singles, U.S. players triumphed seven times while Czech Ivan Lendl captured three championships. Between them, Martina Navratilova, Chris Evert, and Tracy Austin won nine women's singles crowns. Czech Hana Mandlikova would reach the summit in 1985.

The players had their adjustments to make to the Louis Armstrong Stadium. The noise from planes coming and going at nearby LaGuardia Airport created distractions. Those already accustomed to hard surfaces preferred the Deco Turf II, the Center's new surface, over grass or clay. Some clay specialists, such as Borg, were to find the Deco Turf II frustrating. Others, including soft-surface champions such as Evert, adjusted well.

The purse at the U.S. Open had become substantial, making the matches at the National Tennis Center a competitor's dream. Some feared that the major tournament, in its move from Forest Hills to Flushing Meadows Park, would lose its traditions. No one could ever argue, however, that the U.S. Open had lost its excitement. There would be, at the National Tennis Center, thrilling tennis. The 1978–80 era gave tennis a "brand new" beginning and a broad national appeal. As Hester said, "Our game apparently knows no end in its growth and development . . . The strength of tennis is the involvement of people on all levels of interest."

LEFT: Jimmy Connors.

35

Jimmy Connors (left) and
Bjorn Borg pose at the
net prior to the 1978 men's
singles finals.

1978: Any Surface Will Do

Playing championship tennis on grass can be tricky. Winning on clay takes patience. But gaining victory on a hard surface requires mastery of a fast game. Many agree that the mark of a true tennis champion is the mastery of all types of courts.

For Americans such as Jimmy Connors and Chris Evert, any surface will do. In 1978 both of them had the chance to show their virtuoso status. A former UCLA All-American, Connors first had to survive a 4–6, 6–4, 6–1, 1–6, 7–5 fourth round scare from Italy's Adriano Panatta, but he found his game and his spirit in the unexpectedly demanding match. He rang up a decisive victory against Brian Gottfried, 6–2, 7–6, 6–1, and shot past the fast-rising 19-year-old John McEnroe, 6–2, 6–2, 6–4, in the semi-finals. The finals of this U.S. Open gave Connors the chance to claim the U.S. Open title on three surfaces, by defeating Borg. Connors had already won the 1974 U.S. Open on a grass surface and the 1976 U.S. Open on clay. Now he was to prove himself equal to the harder Deco Turf II.

Borg had dazzled the fans with his intimidating serve, his swiftness in covering the court, and his mastery of topspin, both forehand and back-hand. His ability to play his best when coming from behind distinguished his play. Earlier that year he had annihilated Connors in the Wimbledon finals in three sets. However, the Louis Armstrong Stadium proved much faster than the Forest Hills clay surface, making it difficult for him to maneuver successfully.

Borg had run through Bob Hewitt, Heinz Gunthardt, Bernie Mitton, Harold Solomon, Raul Ramirez, and Vitas Gerulaitis in earlier rounds before developing a blister on the thumb of his racket hand. "It made no difference," Borg said of his bandaged thumb. His coach, Lennart Bergelin, had a different opinion. "It was obvious that it was bothering him. He was in pain. You could see that." Borg twice lost his grip on the racket in the match against Connors.

Connors broke Borg's serve early and often in the three-set match. He beat Borg 6–4, 6–2, 6–2 by hitting with blazing velocity. He put his entire body into most of his shots, almost appearing airborne. He seemed to "explode" on the ball.

Following the 1978 triumph, Connors told reporters, "I don't know if I've ever put on so much pressure in a match for so long." Borg said, "Connors was born on an asphalt-like court. There wasn't much I could do, he was at the top of his game." That match, called a "masterpiece of aggression," was truly one of Connors' top achievements. At the age of 26, he had played in his fifth straight U.S. Open final and won three times.

The 1978 U.S. Open gave Evert a similar opportunity to prove her ability to conquer all surfaces. By 1978, Evert had won two French Open titles on clay. In 1974 and 1976, she had triumphed on the grass at Wimbledon. This tournament marked her first on the hard surface after winning three U.S. Opens in a row. Her final match was set against Pam Shriver, the tall sixteen-year-old serve-and-volley specialist.

Shriver had dealt a stunning upset to Martina Navratilova in the semifinals. After winning the first set 7–6, Shriver gained confidence during two rain delays, 48 and 30 minutes apiece in the second set. After play resumed, Pam served well with five aces, 13 winners total, to win the second set, 7–6. She had made few mistakes—two unforced errors in all. She became the youngest woman to play for a U.S. Open title.

LEFT: Chris Evert.

ABOVE: Evert holds win-
ning trophy after beating
Pam Shriver in the 1978
women's singles finals.
It was Evert's fourth
straight U.S. Open
championship.

Despite Shriver's earlier strength, Evert had a date with history. She outsteadied the blitzing Shriver, hit more backhand and forehand winners (24) than Shriver, won 18 points at the net after strong approaches, and never lagged. She clinched the title with a score of 7–5, 6–4. After a stunning debut at the 1971 U.S. Open at the age of 16, Chris Evert had become the "Queen of Tennis," as the first woman to win four straight U.S. Open championships since Helen Jacobs (1932–35) and Molla Bjurstedt (1915–18).

The doubles matches were equally dramatic. In men's doubles Californians Stan Smith and Bob Lutz won their third Men's Open doubles championship by defeating Marty Riessen and Sherwood Stewart. Martina Navratilova and Billie Jean King, both upstaged for the singles title, captured the women's doubles crown. Betty Stove and Frew McMillan walked away with the mixed doubles championship.

1979: Start of Run for Two

Rolling Hills, California and Douglaston, New York may seem worlds apart, but despite differences in weather, tradition, and even the speech of their citizens, they speak the same language when it comes to their athletes—the language of love. Both communities have fostered their athletic programs, proudly contributing stars to sports and entertainment. Both form important components of major entertainment centers: Los Angeles and New York City.

In 1979, when Douglaston's John McEnroe and Rolling Hills' Tracy Austin won the men's and women's championships, the pair began a run of success. Austin would defeat Chris Evert on September 9 to become the youngest United States national singles champion ever at 16 years, 8 months, and 28 days. Previously Maureen Connolly, at 16 years and 11 months, had earned that distinction in 1951.

The third-seeded Austin had defeated Navratilova four times in 15 matches, but never outdoors. In the semifinals, she dramatically upset the second-seeded Navratilova 7–5, 7–5, by playing with aggression and winning despite the necessity to play comeback. In each set she produced winners to give her the final edge.

Austin played just as confidently and just as consistently against Evert. She let Evert make the mistakes. Patiently, she matched her stroke for stroke. The two-fisted backhand artists were both fighting for a place in the record books. Chris, already tied with Jacobs and Bjurstedt with four consecutive U.S. Open women's titles, could have added another claim that would have been tough to beat for some time. But it was the young Austin's day, as an approving National Tennis Center sellout crowd and a world television audience looked on at her 6–4, 6–3 victory. Two champions, two recordholders, but only one could win.

Austin's triumph over Evert proved two things. She could outhit the best baseline player in the women's game, using a similar playing style, and she could take winning the U.S. Open title in stride. "This is the happiest day of my life," Austin told reporters, explaining that Evert earned her admiration in 1974 when she won at Wimbledon at the age of 19.

The men's matches also offered the fans surprises and suspense. In the quarterfinals Bjorn Borg faced super-server Roscoe Tanner. Borg was confident of a win, having recently bested the rocket-launching Tanner in

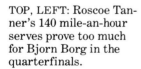

TOP, LEFT: Roscoe Tanner's 140 mile-an-hour serves prove too much for Bjorn Borg in the quarterfinals.

TOP, RIGHT: Tournament referee, Mike Blanchard, discusses a fine point in the rules with Ilie Nastase (left) and John McEnroe.

CENTER, LEFT: McEnroe deposits check for winning the 1979 men's singles title.

CENTER RIGHT: McEnroe discusses pregame strategy with dad.

RIGHT: McEnroe celebrates his victory as runner-up Vitas Gerulaitis walks off the court.

the Wimbledon men's finals. But Tanner had taken the world's top ranked player to five sets before losing the prestigious crown.

This quarterfinal, to Borg's disadvantage, was at night. Returning Tanner's 140 mile-an-hour serves had proven hard enough in daylight. Borg's coach, Bergelin, complained openly and often to the media and anyone else who would listen: "This is not tennis . . . one can not see at night." This time, Borg had the Deco Turf II against him, a surface which allowed balls to bounce much higher than on Wimbledon's grass. The cool weather and Tanner's soaring confidence added to Borg's battle.

Tanner was the victor; the numbers were 6–2, 4–6, 6–2, 7–6. He broke the net with one "monster" delivery and offered 11 aces and 17 service winners. What is more—his overall game had improved. Tanner had unlocked a door to discover the mysteries of Borg's game, and Borg was blocked from a second tennis Grand Slam.

Riding this unexpected victory to the semifinals, Tanner appeared to be making strides against Vitas Gerulaitis in the semifinals. He was up 6–3, 6–2 when Gerulaitis found his game and prevailed in the next three sets 7–6, 6–3, 6–3.

John McEnroe entered the finals match backed by rave reviews from his Stanford University days. At Palo Alto he became only the third United States freshman college player to win the National Collegiate Athletic Association (NCAA) singles championship. (Jimmy Connors and Billy Martin were the other two.)

A year earlier in the 1978 U.S. Open, McEnroe had suffered a 6–2, 6–2, 7–5 semifinal loss to Connors. This time, though, McEnroe won easily over Connors in the semifinals, 6–3, 6–3, 7–5.

With determination as well as a blistering serve-and-volley style, McEnroe downed fellow New Yorker Vitas Gerulaitis 7–5, 6–3, 6–3 on September 9, gaining the first of his three U.S. Open titles. In the finals against Gerulaitis, McEnroe brought out an overpowering serve. Gerulaitis managed only 21 points during McEnroe's 15 service games. The champion served well, volleyed even better, and varied his shot selection intelligently throughout. Gerulaitis, depending most on speed, fell short of his desired achievement.

Young McEnroe cut a striking figure with that victory. He was the youngest male winner of a U.S. national singles championship since 1948, when Pancho Gonzales pulled off the feat at age 20.

McEnroe went on, with his tall partner Peter Fleming, to win the men's doubles championship. Betty Stove again won the double championship, this time with Wendy Turnbull as partner, while Greer Stevens and Bob Hewitt took first place in the mixed doubles competition.

1980: Chris and Mac Get Through

In the yearly quest for the U.S. Open crown, old contenders and new challengers meet. They begin new battles, some of which may last for years. They also duel in grand style, until one survivor decisively walks from the field of battle, exhausted, perhaps having proven his point.

In 1980 McEnroe would play what would have been the match of his life against Borg, a royal match lasting four hours. Also Evert would again assert her ownership of the title "Queen of Tennis." Her fifth win of the

TOP: Another year without a victory at the U.S. Open. Bjorn Borg must think he is jinxed.

RIGHT: John McEnroe's powerful serve was too much for Borg in the 1980 finals.

OVERLEAF, LEFT: Borg launches another lethal backhand down the line.

OVERLEAF, RIGHT: Borg was blessed with exceptional quickness and speed.

Open title would shoot her over great women players of the past, such as Helen Jacobs, Elisabeth Moore, Hazel Hotchkiss Wightman, Alice Marble, Billie Jean King, Maria Bueno, and Pauline Betz, all of whom had captured four crowns. This triumph would also put her closer to the company of Helen Wills Moody and Margaret Smith Court, with their seven and five titles respectively, and Molla Bjurstedt Mallory, with eight titles.

Borg's journey to the finals had required him to overcome Roscoe Tanner, the player with the legendary cannon serve. This time the quarterfinal match took place in daylight, but Tanner's bullets were still hard to fight. Tanner scored 19 aces and 28 service winners. Down 4–2 in the fourth set after scores of 6–4, 3–6, and 4–6, Borg had to defend his kingdom. He smashed three returns for winners off second serves. He had found himself, at 3–4, then 4–all. The fans would see again why Borg had been called "the best," better than Budge, Gonzales, Tilden, Laver, et. al.

"When I got down, 4–2, I felt Roscoe, being the guy ahead, would get a little tight. He has to take a few more chances. I just told myself, 'You have nothing to lose right now,' " Borg reported. Tanner disagreed, but he added, "Borg made a great comeback. But it's in the fifth set when he turns on the speed." Borg did take the last two sets, 7–5, 6–3.

Many felt this was the U.S. Open that Borg would finally call his own. McEnroe felt differently. "I know I have to serve well to have a chance," he said. He was ready for the challenge. He had squeaked past Connors in the semifinals 6–4, 5–7, 0–6, 6–3, 7–6. Borg had just disposed of a future giant—Ivan Lendl, by a 4–6, 6–3, 6–2, 7–5 count. It had not been easy. A serious contender for the Grand Slam since 1974, Borg had become tired of falling short of one Grand Slam event—the U.S. Open. Earlier that summer, McEnroe had clashed with Borg in a spectacular Wimbledon final match and Borg emerged the victor. Borg had already won 13 straight matches of the five-set variety, beginning in 1976.

The finals match began at 4:12 p.m. and was not over until 8:23 p.m. The attendance swelled to 20,171, and Borg's drained fans never gave up hope. Undaunted, McEnroe offered sharp serves the entire evening, while Borg did not serve well and made many unforced errors. Borg hadn't quite found his rhythm in the first set, but he broke McEnroe, at love, and led 5–4. Serving for the set, he went 3-for-6 in the first serve department, and McEnroe broke back. After two deuces and a controversial call against McEnroe, Borg led, 6–5. Two double faults and three bad forehands following, Borg discovered he was at a disheartening 6–6. In the tiebreaker, McEnroe, sensing opportunity, pounded away and cleared his first hurdle. This was the first set—McEnroe, 7–6 (7–3).

Dropping 13 straight points and missing his first serve 14 of 22 times, Borg fell 6–1 in the second set. No one knew what was wrong. It seemed Borg was simply in shock.

In search of his second U.S. Open Crown, McEnroe, only 21 years old, thereupon let up. Fatigue may have been a factor, along with inexperience, but this mistake proved a steep one. McEnroe's serves became vulnerable, and Borg leaped on them. Just when Borg appeared again in possession of his game, however, serving for the third set at 5–4, he was able to manage only 3 of 5 first serves. Bouncing back, McEnroe took the set to 5–all and then took a 6–5 lead before his swift foe carded an ace and

49

"Right then, I felt like my body would drop off."

held serve at 6–all. Borg won the tiebreaker at 7–5 on a high backhand volley miss-hit by McEnroe.

Deprived of the serve that had once been described as "enormous," Borg exhibited considerable savvy and backbone in the fourth set. With great speed on the court, he smashed winners that few players at any age have in their repertoires. Borg went 20-for-25 in points-won-on-serve category. He won set four 7–5 by breaking McEnroe following four deuces, when he reached back and stunned his opponent with two sizzling passing shots off return of service. One went down the line, and the other was classic Borg—a booming backhand crosscourt hit at a sharp angle.

At 3–3 in the fifth set, all seemed well for Borg, while not so good for McEnroe, until a controversial line call and two double faults put McEnroe ahead at 4–3. "I know many people felt that a bad call was my undoing, but I didn't serve well," Borg told the media following the match. McEnroe served out the match 6–4, and Borg, once more, left the U.S. Open without the opportunity to clench a Grand Slam in December in Australia.

Prior to the fifth set, McEnroe said he was "exhausted and was in trouble. I was really tired, and I knew Bjorn just gets stronger as a match goes on. Right then, I felt like my body would drop off." But he had faced such a dilemma before. "Mental toughness can allow you to hang in there," said Peter Fleming, McEnroe's doubles partner.

Chris Evert was able to avenge her loss in the 1979 U.S. Open finals to Tracy Austin this year. She eliminated Austin from the tournament in the semifinals, winning 4–6, 6–1, 6–1. This was a match that Evert claimed she "wanted more than any other," and a win that may have been the most emotional for her thus far.

Hana Mandlikova arrived at the finals after overpowering Andrea Jaeger in the semifinals. She broke out swiftly in the championship match and took first set honors 7–5. But Evert bounced back with a winning lob and two crosscourt forehands, then coasted to her fifth Open championship with sets of 6–1, 6–1. "I really didn't feel like I had my rhythm the whole match because Hana never hits the same shot twice in a row," said Evert, adding "Hana has really played unbelievably the past few weeks. I'm sure she'll be a future champion." Evert, who had taken a few months off before returning to win 42 of 43 matches, expressed considerable gratitude to her family after this special match.

This was an historic year for other reasons. Bob Lutz and Stan Smith won their fourth U.S. Open men's doubles championship against John McEnroe and Peter Fleming. Martina Navratilova, who had lost to Evert, won the women's doubles title with Billie Jean King. Wendy Turnbull and Marty Riessen wrapped up the mixed doubles match.

4 *1981–1983: Americans, Moving Fast*

The seas on which a player charts his or her course to the U.S. Open finals, or any championship match for that matter, are seldom calm ones. Even the finest players, already champions, find themselves fiercely navigating storms. Injury, illness, aging, and even personal temperament—all these show the public the athlete at his most vulnerable and human moments.

During these years, Americans watched their athletes, flaws and strengths both evident, reveal the qualities necessary to outlast defeat and to capture victory. John McEnroe, Jimmy Connors, Chris Evert, and Tracy Austin, already proven winners, would win U.S. Open singles championships in 1981, 1982, and 1983.

Others had won major tennis titles at the age of 30 or older. Admittedly, they are the exceptions, but players such as Jimmy Connors never claimed to be merely mortal. Married with a young son, Connors appeared in 1982 at the age of 30 to be content with life. Positive mental outlook alone does not guarantee winning status for even a great player, but when a great player also finds a new serve he sometimes gets his way. He had won the crown in 1974, 1976, and 1978, and he thought it was his turn again. He would win in 1982 and 1983. At the end of the 1983 U.S. Open Connors had charted a notable course for himself as winner of five U.S. Opens, the most since Tilden's post-World War I era record.

McEnroe had won successive crowns in 1979 and 1980, and would win again in 1981, guaranteeing himself a place in tennis history. His three consecutive wins likewise evoked references to Tilden, who won six straight championships in the 1920s. No one else in between won more than two straight top honors among the men's singles players, although Vines, Budge, Riggs, Kramer could have if they had not turned pro.

Although Evert had already asserted her excellence with five U.S. Open titles, she was denied a victory in her final round try at the 1981 U.S. Open, as Austin would pick up her second title that year. Austin, however, would drop off the women's pro circuit tour soon because of injury. She had played well, at the ages of 16 and 18, first as the youngest champion ever to win a U.S. national singles crown and then overcoming injury to triumph.

LEFT: Master of the serve, John McEnroe serves up another ace.

1981: Centenary Exercises

The hundredth anniversary of the USTA left the fans with plenty to think about. Navratilova and Evert faced each other in a match of pure skills, while McEnroe, with his great second serve and his agile ways on

1981 U.S. Open

Past U.S. singles champions were honored during ceremonies on center court at the Centennial U.S. Open in 1981.

FRONT ROW (l to r): USTA President Marvin Richmond; Tracy Austin (1979, '81); Maria Bueno (1959, '63, '64, '66); Althea Gibson (1957, '58); Sarah Palfrey Danzig (1941, '45); Shirley Fry Irvin (1956); Margaret Osborne duPont (1948, '49, '50); Pauline Betz Addie (1942, '43, '44, '46).

BACK ROW: (l to r): Rod Laver (1962, '69); Tony Trabert (1953, '55); Arthur Ashe (1968); Fred Stolle (1966); Art Larsen (1950); Vic Seixas (1954); Jack Kramer (1946, '47); Ellsworth Vines (1931, '32); Fred Perry (1933, '34, '36); Jimmy Connors (1974, '76, '78); Frank Parker (1944, '45).

hard courts, took his place in the history books. Even the men's doubles had their moment.

Evert had scored a 6–1, 6–3 quarterfinal victory against Mandlikova. Her next match, with Navratilova, was electrically charged. At first she was slow to the ball and lacked crispness; she fell behind 5–2, pushed by Navratilova's serve and sharp volleys. But she hit three consecutive winners to tie the first set at 5–all. Navratilova, behind a strong first serve and two Evert unforced errors, jumped up 6–5, taking the set at 7–5.

Combining drop shots with bothersome lobs and deep and precise service returns, Evert took a 3–1 lead in the second set. Navratilova held and broke back with a superb passing shot to even it 3–all. Evert's accurate forehand winners finally prevailed to tie the match with a 6–4 set.

The tied match delivered more drama, as Evert took an early 3–1 lead. Navratilova hit three winners past her foe for 4–all. Leading 15–40, Evert saw two backhands wane, one too wide and one too deep. In the next game, Evert serving and down 4–5, she double-faulted at deuce. A forehand winner saved one match point, but that was it. Her backhand lob landed long off a Navratilova volley, and the Czech player had made the finals in the first of her six U.S. Open championship final appearances between 1981 and 1987.

Austin was waiting—this time two years older. She had made a comeback from a lower back injury, becoming more aware of the work necessary for another crown, not to mention the effort required to overcome Navratilova, in the process.

The match lasted two hours and 40 minutes. Using the 12-point tiebreaker, this match marked the first time tiebreakers would determine a woman's U.S. Open singles championship.

Navratilova had her chances. In the second set, double break point went by the wayside due to her own errors. Serving not for the match but to tie, she later had three occasions at deuce to straighten her game out. The second set tiebreak found two Navratilova forehands out of step, one long and one in the net. Austin then had the edge.

The third set was close and could have gone either way, for Navratilova continually hit deep backhands and charged the net. Although fearing Navratilova's famous forehand, Austin suddenly smashed three forehands to Navratilova's forehand side, catching her by complete surprise. This gave her a 1–0 edge in the decisive third set. Then arrived an unusual event—a match-deciding double fault by the challenger.

"I had to come back from an injury, and I didn't realize quite what I had accomplished when I won the U.S. Open in 1979," said Austin. "This was the best!" Very simply, consistent steady play had enabled Austin to win her second U.S. Open crown, stopping Navratilova, 1–6, 7–6, 7–6.

John McEnroe was seeking his third U.S. Open championship in succession. To do it, he would have to deny Bjorn Borg the finals honor once more.

Borg started fast, precisely homing in on 72 percent of his first serves. He claimed the first set 6–4. McEnroe jumped on what seemed a Borg letup, rolling through set two 6–2. Breaking service and holding his own, Borg went up 4–2 in the third before McEnroe stormed back to 3–4 and then 4–all with two great crosscourt backhand passes and a pair of

ABOVE: Tracy Austin hits
her consistent two-handed
backhand on the way to her
second U.S. Open victory.

RIGHT: Austin, making a
comeback from a lower
back injury, stretches for
a running forehand in her
1–6, 7–6, 7–6 win over
Martina Navratilova.

incomparable topspin lobs. "That was one of the best games I've played against someone else's serve in a long time," McEnroe told reporters.

Borg tried desperately to hold on, but at 4–5 McEnroe watched a Borg forehand run long before chewing up a forehand crosscourt winning chance to go up. Down 2–3 in the fourth set, Borg smacked two bad backhands and two disobedient forehands to lose 6–3 in the fourth set.

McEnroe's play confused Borg with a variety of spins, variations in speed, and great anticipation. He would never win the U.S. Open and the Swedish player seemed old at the age of 25 at 0-for-4 in the U.S. Open singles final. McEnroe, at 22, had the crown and his third U.S. Open championship in succession.

During the men's doubles semifinals, spectators witnessed an event that some thought represented the changing spirit of tennis. It was a timely reminder of the difference between professional tennis, with its competitive edge, and the older amateur play, with its sporting side.

"The young Americans had to get by the Australians first. It was difficult."

The game the fans would remember took place between Australians Fred Stolle and John Newcombe and their American adversaries John McEnroe and Peter Fleming. Stolle and Newcombe each had won an U.S. Open singles titles, with Stolle taking the ascent in 1966 over Newcombe, 4–6, 12–10, 6–3, 6–4, and Newcombe leaving victorious in 1967 and 1973. Each of the Australians had to his credit three doubles titles in U.S. Open men's play. Stolle, at 43, and Newcombe, at 37, had been serious contenders for the 1981 doubles championship, but they had not been so much in the limelight for quite some time.

Fleming, 26, and McEnroe had taken the 1978 men's doubles title and would eventually prevail in 1981, this time over Heinz Gunthardt and Peter McNamara (by default). However, the young Americans had to get by the Australians first. It was difficult.

The two-on-two followed Borg's exciting quarterfinal triumph over Tanner. The crowd "hung around," curious for a glimpse of four doubles masters. They stayed longer than they had planned.

Early on, everything seemed in place. The younger players led at first, and then, boom! McEnroe blasted Stolle with an up-close volley. The ball hit the New South Wales native on the neck. Newcombe was furious.

"A shot like that could have put out Fred's eye," he said. "There were two balls hit at me like that, one at my head and one at my crotch. . . . I feel sorry for them [the players] both. In our day, we never forgot it was a [gentleman's] sport."

Stolle added, "The game used to be a lot more bloody fun. That's why you see us old guys out here playing whilst we can still enjoy it a bit. I'll wager there's not many of the top 10 players today who will be playing when they're 43."

The crowd got into it. And the majority overwhelmingly backed the Australians. Fired up, Stolle and Newcombe took sets three and four by scores of 7–5 and 7–6. However, McEnroe and Fleming edged past their older rivals 7–6 (7–3).

"When you're hitting a ball 100 miles an hour, it's ridiculous to say you're deliberately trying to hit someone," said Fleming after the game. "It's just not valid."

65

ALL: John McEnroe.

TOP, LEFT: John McEnroe
returns shot to veterans
Fred Stolle (right) and
John Newcombe in the
men's doubles semifinals.
He and Peter Fleming
went on to win 4–6, 12–10,
6–3, 6–3.

BOTTOM, LEFT: Anne
Smith (center) and Kathy
Jordan share the women's
doubles trophy.

"I can't win either way," said McEnroe, who was upset and didn't take kindly to Newcombe's remarks. "If I talk, I'm wrong. And if I don't, people will think I'm wrong."

"Different days, different kinds of people," concluded Newcombe. McEnroe and Fleming, immensely competitive. Stolle and Newcombe, sporting sorts. Each generation had something to say, a statement to make.

The other 1981 doubles champions were Kathy Jordan and Anne Smith, winning over Rosemary Casals and Wendy Turnbull, and Anne Smith and Kevin Curren, edging past JoAnne Russell and Steve Denton for the mixed doubles title.

1982: Holding off a Practically New European Blast

Ivan Lendl's savage forehand, almost legendary, had enabled him to post a 117–7 record since the 1981 U.S. Open. His impressive rise included 11 of 18 tournament victories, and he had been a finalist in 16 of those. He met fierce competition in the form of John McEnroe, winner of the last three U.S. Opens, although Mac had lost the Wimbledon finals to Jimmy Connors.

Connors was confident, though aging at 30. "I bet 99.9 percent of people thought that I couldn't be number one, but I thought I could," Connors said, towards the end of the tournament.

It looked like a good tournament. McEnroe had perhaps the best second serve in the game's history. Connors possessed the best return of serve and an improved first serve. Lendl, sometimes a good server, featured a devastating flat, full forehand, best called "overpowering."

Connors wanted more. For the first time since 1969 (the year Rod Laver won his second Grand Slam title), the U.S. Open fans witnessed the tournament's four top-seeded men players making the semifinals. There Connors dropped Guillermo Vilas, attempting to repeat his spectacular 1977 U.S. Open win. Final score—6–1, 3–6, 6–2, 6–3.

Lendl had begun to blow his opponents away, and he would do the same to McEnroe, in his own fashion, in the semifinals. He took the three-time defending champion out 6–4, 6–4, 7–6.

Entering the match with an 8–1 winning mark against Lendl, Connors appeared assured. Having slept little the night before, Lendl exhibited anxiety, despite having won over 80 percent of his first service points against McEnroe in the semifinals.

Constantly pressuring Lendl's backhand, Connors broke him four times. The challenger would only succeed with half of his first serves the first three sets. In contrast, Connors was sharp, making good 77 percent and then 65 percent of his first serves in the semifinals and the finals. He kept his foe off-balance with deep and low returns and won set four by going to the net at almost every good opportunity. Connors, who made few errors, only let up somewhat in set three when Lendl capitalized on his own serve.

Connors won his fourth U.S. Open in 1982 by overcoming Lendl 6–3, 6–2, 4–6, 6–4. The win put him ahead of such notables as Fred Perry, Malcolm Whitman, Oliver Campbell, and McEnroe in number of U.S. National singles titles captured.

OVERLEAF, LEFT: Ivan
Lendl shows perfect form
on his serve. He won over
eighty percent of his first
service points in defeating
John McEnroe in the
semifinals.

OVERLEAF, RIGHT: Jimmy
Connors kept Lendl
on the run with deep
returns.

BELOW: Ivan Lendl.

RIGHT: Connors holds
winning trophy as runner-
up Lendl looks on.

As for achieving new popularity, Connors told the media that the fans at the U.S. Open "probably feel sorry for an old man running around like me." Lendl had not been beaten by an old man, he felt, but by a fast player of constant motion. Suddenly, the Connors of 1974, 1976, and 1978 had returned, better than most remembered him. Some had thought Connors' best days were behind him.

Apparently few suspected that his finest moments were around the bend. Connors had become more patient, more friendly, and more popular with the years. But his new serve, according to Connors, was victory's most effective weapon.

In the women's semifinals, Mandlikova had shaken up Pam Shriver, 6–4, 2–6, 6–2, and Evert had taught 17 year-old Andrea Jaeger a 6–2, 6–1 lesson. Shriver, who defeated Navratilova in the semifinals to reach the 1978 finals, had beat her new doubles partner in the quarterfinals this year. Navratilova, seeking an elusive Grand Slam, was suffering from toxoplasmosis, a cat virus. Mandlikova had battled 1979 and 1981 champion Austin in the quarterfinals, and two of the top-seeded players were out.

Prior to the finals, Evert had called Mandlikova "unpredictable" and "tough to play," but she made quick work of the two-time U.S. Open finalist from the baseline. Mandlikova, recovering from a back injury, was unable to put away her customary lobs. Evert won the crown in an hour and four minutes with a score of 6–3, 6–1.

Thus the champion set two milestones. First she captured her 66th U.S. Open match victory, surpassing eight-time national champion Molla Bjurstedt Mallory. Second, for the ninth straight year, she walked away with at least one of the Grand Slam titles. No other woman player had done that.

Evert once again reminded the fans that she possessed exceptional skill, as well as her sixth U.S. Open title.

Kevin Curren and Steve Denton defeated Victor Amaya and Hank Pfister, 6–2, 6–7, 5–7, 6–2, 6–4 for the men's doubles finals. Last year's defeated team, Rosemary Casals and Wendy Turnbull, came back to down Sharon Walsh and Barbara Potter, 6–4, 6–4 for the women's doubles title. Anne Smith and Kevin Curren repeated as mixed doubles title winners when they beat Barbara Potter and Ferdi Taygan 6–7, 7–6, 7–6.

1983: Once More/At Last

As if his previous win didn't suffice, Jimmy Connors announced "once more." Martina Navratilova chimed in with "let me try again" at the U.S. Open women's title—the win she wanted so badly.

Before the stars played, the young contenders put on a good show. Bill Scanlon, former NCAA champion, had the biggest surprise. He was returning to the pro tour after a break, under the guidance of Warren Jacques. His unsuspecting victim, John McEnroe, had just won the 1983 Wimbledon title.

To qualify for the quarterfinals, Scanlon gave McEnroe a shocking 7–6, 7–6, 4–6, 6–3 defeat with sharp volleys, deep ground strokes, and a tough tiebreaker attitude.

In the men's quarterfinals, Ivan Lendl succeeded over Mats Wilander, 6–4, 6–4, 7–6, 7–4, while Connors taught a 7–6, 6–2, 6–2 lesson

to Eliot Teltscher. Jimmy Arias edged Yannick Noah, 7–6, 4–6, 6–3, 1–6, 7–5. And finally, Bill Scanlon barely got past Mark Dickson, 3–6, 6–4, 4–6, 6–3, 7–6.

Scanlon offered no surprises in the semifinals for Jimmy Connors whose trademark return of serve was at its peak. He leaped on Scanlon's mistakes, keeping his own hard-hit offerings deep and low.

He volleyed confidently, displaying an excellent overall game. It was Connors over Scanlon, 6–2, 7–6, 7–3, 6–1. In the other men's semifinals, Lendl had confidently prevailed over Arias 6–2, 7–6, 7–3, 6–1.

In the finals match, Lendl chose to remain mostly at the baseline. Both players' services were broken early, and it was 3–3 in the first set. Connors went up, 4–3, and broke Lendl with a combination of strong service returns and deep approaches Lendl couldn't handle. Connors went for four straight points on serve to take the first set.

Lendl got his forehand and backhand going in set two. He captured it, despite Connors' lunges, surges, and quick returns. Ivan took the tie-break, 7–2.

Connors and Lendl took turns serving poorly in the third set, and it was 3–1, Lendl, when the Czechoslovakian player's energy level dropped drastically. The afternoon temperature, more than 100 degrees at courtside, became a significant factor in the game's progress. Sweltering conditions notwithstanding, Connors held sturdy and when Lendl (up an initial ad) double-faulted at 5–4, the left hander put away a volley and played a similar shot to the hilt for a deadlock. Lendl couldn't come back. "After I double-faulted, I never recovered," he said. Connors rolled through the fourth set, as Lendl was obviously exhausted.

Connors intensified his efforts. Lendl swatted from the baseline. It appeared as if he couldn't decide on some balls whether to come in or go back. The final set ended 6–0, and Connors was jubilant. He had won his fifth U.S. Open title.

Navratilova defeated friend and doubles partner Pam Shriver 6–2, 6–1 in the semifinals, drawing on her usual athletic prowess. She was strong, quick, and resourceful that year, requiring barely six total hours of playing time throughout the tournament to win.

Evert had trouble with another serve-and-volley expert, Britain's Jo Durie. Durie, incidentally, was the first British player to reach the U.S. Open semifinals since Virginia Wade in 1975. Although she was charged with 26 unforced errors, Durie nevertheless proved a solid competitor for Evert. Durie tried to use her 5-foot-11 frame to a distinct advantage. For a while she did, but then she began to bang volleys into the net. The final score was a close 6–4, 6–4.

A regal sum of $120,000 awaited the champion, but it was finally reaching the top that meant most to Navratilova. In the previous 20 months, she had produced an impressive 156–4 record in matches played— a winning percentage of .975.

It had been a good 10 years since Navratilova and Evert's initial confrontation. In her encounters with the great player, Navratilova gained ground rapidly. Evert had posted a 23–3 initial advantage over her adversary, but the pendulum had swung in the opposite direction recently by a 21–7 persuasion. Navratilova entered the title match with a 65–1 showing

*Lendl: "After I
double-faulted, I
never recovered."*

ABOVE & RIGHT: Chris Evert's solid ground game was not enough to produce another championship win in 1983.

ABOVE: Martina Navrati-
lova's game matures and
she captures her first U.S.
Open crown.

"Navratilova had finally triumphed after 11 years of aiming for the zenith."

for 1983. She had dropped only a solitary skirmish to Kathy Horvath on clay in the Paris tournaments. Evert held the edge by a 7–0 tally over Navratilova in clay matches, but the Flushing Meadows' Deco Turf II surface gave play a different character.

Martina's attacks drove home 72.5 percent of her first serves, and she was crisp in the forecourt. The result was a convincing 6–1, 6–3 verdict in the challenger's favor. This was Navratilova's 35th tournament triumph in the past three years. She had prevailed in four Wimbledons, one French, and one Australian, and now she finally had the U.S. Open title.

This match raised anew the question of which player would be judged the better of the pair and how the duo would finally rate against other stalwarts of the sport.

"If I can stay healthy, I don't think there will be any arguments. I know I'll be up there," said the winner. "You're dealing with pride here" Chris had told reporters. "She's got to play at this level for another five or six years to prove herself."

The six-time U.S. Open titleholder revealed that she thought comparisons to other players—Helen Wills, Billie Jean King—weren't all that valid. Different times, different players, she granted.

For the time being, however, there was no doubt. A runner, basketball *aficionado*, an incredible athlete, Navratilova had finally triumphed after 11 years of aiming for the zenith.

Australians Elizabeth Sayers and John Fitzgerald won in mixed doubles against Barbara Potter and Ferdi Taygan, 3–6, 6–3, 6–4. Shriver and an energized Navratilova took the match in women's doubles over Rosalyn Fairbank and Candy Reynolds, 6–7, 6–1, 6–3. Finally, Peter Fleming and John McEnroe beat Fritz Buehning and Van Winitsky in men's doubles, 6–3, 6–4, 6–2.

ABOVE & RIGHT: Jimmy Connors.

95

older, they [sic] gave them [the tennis players] more equipment and more
possibility to play."

Hana Mandlikova, trained by the Prague Sparta Club, followed in
Martina Navratilova's footsteps. The next Czech wave includes Miloslav
Mecir, Milan Srejber, and Helena Sukova.

Bjorn Borg, of course, was gone from the professional circuit by the
mid-1980s. However, an impressive "ensuing assembly" of Swedes arrived
in the 1984–1986 term. They included Mats Wilander, Stefan Edberg,
Joakim Nystrom, and Anders Jarryd.

The German Boris Becker won Wimbledon at 17 in 1985, quickly
becoming a star. Millions became excited about him. They fell in love with
his dives, lunges, and hustle as well as his enthusiastic style and desire
to win. Naturally he headed a list of talented contenders from West
Germany, including Steffi Graf.

During the last several years, France has offered some splendid
players: Yannick Noah, Henri Leconte, Guy Forget, and Catherine
Tanvier.

Rod Laver and his mates—Ken Rosewall, Fred Stolle, John
Newcombe, Neale Fraser, Tony Roche, Frank Sedgman, Roy Emerson and
Lewis Hoad—did much to make the world believe the best tennis players
came from Australia, from the early 1950s through the early 1970s.

Thus, when Australian John Fitzgerald paired with Czech Tomas
Smid to defeat Stefan Edberg and Anders Jarryd in the 1984 U.S. Open
men's doubles title match, many said it felt good to see an Australian again
triumphant.

Americans had also begun experiencing a "changing of the guard"
by late 1986. Evert, who had made the U.S. Open semifinals an unprece-
dented 16 times, was still considered Navratilova's chief competition. However, Mandlikova, Steffi Graf, and Helena Sukova were exhibiting strength.
Jimmy Connors was still ranked in the world's top 10, but John McEnroe
lost his standing in that league after taking some time away from the game
for fatherhood and marriage.

The Swedish-West German-Czechoslovak connection threatened to
overtake the American's dominance of the game, however, by the end of
the 1984–1986 period.

With McEnroe, Connors, and Evert getting older, Americans
remained on the lookout for new native players to keep the proud tradition
alive. Americans are never too far from being the world's best, and they
rarely like for anyone else to lay claim to their territory for long. Connors,
Evert, and McEnroe, great champions all, weren't about to quit, either.

1984: Super Saturday

Saturday, September 8, 1984 will certainly rank as highly in the eyes of
Open sports fans as any in the past or any in the future. It was a marathon
tennis fan's kind of day. Beginning at about 11 o'clock in the morning, a
little more than 12 hours would pass before two men's semifinals, the
women's title match, and a 35-and-over men's semifinal attraction—pitting
popular Stan Smith against equally well-liked John Newcombe—had been
completed.

Prior to the legendary Saturday play, Australian Pat Cash's quarterfinal upset of Sweden's Mats Wilander (7–6, 6–4, 2–6, 6–3) distin-

97

guished him as the first male Australian semifinalist in a decade. In other quarterfinal play, Lendl whipped fifth-seeded Andres Gomez of Ecuador 6–4, 6–4, 6–1. Connors beat Evert's husband, John Lloyd, who played better than the 7–5, 6–2, 6–0 score represented. And McEnroe outbattled Gene Mayer 7–5, 6–3, 6–4.

But everything paled against the tennis played on that memorable Saturday. Stan Smith and John Newcombe warmed the fans up with a thriller. Smith pulled it out 4–6, 7–5, 6–2, then went on to beat Marty Riessen for top honors on Sunday. The duration of this match threw the two men's semifinals and the women's final behind schedule. The players grumbled, but McEnroe commented, "That had to be the greatest day for U.S. Open fans . . . ever."

The men's semifinals matched Lendl against Cash and Connors opposite McEnroe. Both battles would go five sets. In a match that took 54 games to complete, Lendl outlasted Cash in an encounter lasting three hours, 39 minutes. The 19-year-old Melbourne native lost to Lendl because he could not put away his volley smashes persuasively enough. Nevertheless, his play served notice that he would be a force to reckon with on the court. Lendl took the honors 3–6, 6–3, 6–4, 6–7, 7–6.

Previously declaring the U.S. Open the tournament the one he most wanted to win, Connors was ready to play. He was to break McEnroe's serve seven times, his fierce return of service in an ever-sharp state. McEnroe's uncharacteristic baseline game took Connors in set three and his strong serve-volley game prevailed in set five. Connors recorded 45 winners, while McEnroe tallied 20. The Long Island lefty had his dazzling serve at work and he registered 19 aces. McEnroe leaped to a 3–0 lead in the fifth set, destroying Connors' hopes for a sixth U.S. Open victory by a 6–4, 4–6, 7–5, 4–6, 6–3 spread. The match took three hours and 45 minutes, stretching for 51 games.

> *"New Yorkers love it when you spill your guts out there."*

"New Yorkers love it when you spill your guts out there," said Connors. "You spill your guts out at Wimbledon, [and] they make you stop and clean it up."

Lendl never had a chance against McEnroe in the title match, as the southpaw charged the net 54 times. He made good on 37 points or 68.5 percent of his shots.

"I thought I was hitting the ball well," Lendl told reporters after the clash. "But in order to play even or beat him, you have to return his serve and break him too." Lendl became the first man since Bill Johnston (1925) to lose three U.S. finals in a row, but the right-handed ace would have his day to shine in the sun.

This U.S. Open championship was the fourth for McEnroe. The 25 year-old left hander joined the ranks of great players who had won four or more U.S. National singles titles—Robert Wrenn, William Larned, Jimmy Connors, Richard Sears, and Bill Tilden.

One thing had changed. Following an outburst at the French Open, the usually feisty McEnroe resolved to let his tennis speak for him. The change of strategy worked, giving him the energy necessary to triumph once again in New York.

McEnroe, mellowing and hopeful of more popularity and acceptance than ever before, was even more humorous on the court at times.

ABOVE, LEFT: Pat Cash, a consistent net rusher, made his first semifinal appearance at the U.S. Open but lost to Ivan Lendl.

ABOVE: Martina Navratilova's aggressive style wins her another championship.

ABOVE: Stan Smith (left)
beat John Newcombe
in the 35 and over
semifinals.

LEFT: John McEnroe.

After questioning one call, he declared, "Ah, go grow some hair," to a linesman who had none. In other years, he might have spoken more strongly.

Said McEnroe after winning: "I feel tired; I feel really exhausted. I feel unbelievable and terrible at the same time. My body said 'that's enough,' but the fact that I was tired made me concentrate better. The more tired I felt, the better I thought I hit the ball. It was a mental thing—push, push—and I didn't get angry at anything, because I needed every ounce of energy I had."

The women's quarterfinals combined surprise with charm. Canada's Carling Bassett, billed "sometime model, sometime actress, full-time tennis pro," bumped off third-seeded Mandlikova, 6–4, 6–3. The 16 year-old Bassett got that far despite a case of laryngitis. She fell to Chris in the semifinals 6–2, 6–2, but she added beauty, enthusiasm, and some very good tennis to the tournament. Australian Wendy Turnbull pulled the other quarterfinal surprise when she upended fourth-seeded Pam Shriver 2–6, 6–3, 6–3.

To make it to the semifinals a record 14th year in a row, Chris Evert defeated Sylvia Hanika of West Germany 6–2, 6–3. Playing quarter-finals amid nighttime swirling winds, Martina Navratilova won against Helena Sukova 6–3, 6–3. To have a chance of winning the crown twice in a row, Navratilova knew she would have to get past Wendy Turnbull in the semifinals. She did, 6–4, 6–4.

Entering the finals, Evert stood 50–7 for the year, while Navratilova's mark held forth at an almost incomparable 52–1. Navratilova had her way in the first set. Chris, waiting for the right moment to put as much psycho-logical pressure as possible on Navratilova, finally got her chance in the second set. Navratilova was up a break at 4–3 and it was 0–30. Evert then hit a backhand passing shot wide and that, for all functional purposes, was it.

Navratilova was just busy being Navratilova. Although not playing her best, the tremendously gifted athlete tied Evert's record of 55 matches won in a row when she captured her second consecutive singles title in the 1984 Open.

The triumph was Navratilova's 13th straight over Evert, who said, "It's just not enough to play a good match against her anymore." The final tally was 4–6, 6–4, 6–4. Navratilova would go on to win $2,173,556 in 1984, including the U.S. Open's first prize of $160,000 for the singles champion.

The men's doubles championship was won by John Fitzgerald and Tomas Smid. The Australian-Czechoslovak combination prevailed by a 7–6, 6–3, 6–3 leeway over the Swedish twosome of Stefan Edberg and Anders Jarryd, the eighth-seeded team. They had startled the top-seeded duo of McEnroe and Peter Fleming, 3–6, 7–6, 7–5, 7–6. That match required three hours, 14 minutes. Shriver and Navratilova captured their second straight women's doubles crown by bumping off England's Anne Hobbs and Australia's Wendy Turnbull 6–2, 6–4. Tom Gullikson and Bulgarian Manuela Maleeva narrowly stopped the Sayers-Fitzgerald Australian two-some in the mixed doubles' title final match, 2–6, 7–5, 6–4.

ABOVE: Canada's Carling
Bassett knocked off Hana
Mandlikova to reach her
first U.S. Open semifinal.

LEFT: Carling Bassett.

1985: A Superlative Year

The star of the 1985 U.S. Open was perhaps the biggest surprise of all—the afternoon tornado that uprooted trees, bent fencing, knocked down a party tent, and turned Stadium Court into a pond. It's all in a day's work at the Open, though. Things like hurricanes bring people together, and staff and contractors alike came out in full force (pronto!) to clear the grounds and repair the damage. Other high points: a record total of 409,455 fans witnessed the 1985 U.S. Open, a $2,953,500 tournament. First prize to the singles champs was $187,500 per winner. Imagine these possible superlatives.

- Boris Becker, 17, Wimbledon champ, losing in the round of 16.
- Three tiebreakers deciding a woman's quarterfinal, a first.
- The Swedish coming back despite losing one star.
- Ivan Lendl achieving star status.
- Mandlikova, now 23, taking her place as a champion.

The year was 1985, a superlative year. New York fans had been wishing "en masse" for Becker at least to make the finals, but the dashing West German did not meet their expectations. He had won at Wimbledon over Kevin Curren, but he fell to Joakim Nystrom 6–3, 6–4, 4–6, 6–4 in the round of 16 at the U.S. Open.

Nystrom went on to lose to John McEnroe in the night quarterfinals 6–1, 6–0, 7–5, but the newcomer, along with his fellow countrymen Mats Wilander and Anders Jarryd, proved that Swedish tennis was alive. Jarryd fell to the heat and to Wilander in the quarters.

McEnroe prevailed in the semifinals over excessive humidity and some daring net play by Wilander. With steady groundstrokes he served well in the fourth set and waited for the Swede's usually steady game to fall apart.

Ivan Lendl would be waiting for McEnroe at the finals. He could leave $187,500 richer, having earned the distinction of being the first right-hander to win the U.S. Open men's singles crown since John Newcombe took the honor in 1973. Lendl knew that if he could muster all of his energy and drive, combining them with a much improved net and volley approach, he had an excellent chance to win his first U.S. Open singles crown in four tries as a finalist.

However, first he had to beat Connors. Lendl knew a variety of shots was necessary to offset Connors' practice of returning a ball harder than it had been sent. Adding a backhand slice to his game and changing speeds, Lendl was smarter than in his earlier meetings with Connors. The left hander limped, bothered by an ankle problem. He wasn't as sharp as he could have been, and Lendl insured his own triumph by getting an early jump on his foe and maintaining an upper hand. The final was Lendl, 6–2, 6–3, 7–5.

With his stoic manner and rigid style, Lendl was not a crowd favorite. Against Connors, however, Lendl was cheered for his good play. "They were fair and that was nice," he said of those in attendance. "The first step is to have them admire me." The next step was just to play hard and to play well. "The fans get behind Connors and they like to give me a hard time," Lendl explained. "But this is the tournament I would like to win the most, for my family, because I live in this country now, only 28 miles away."

LEFT: A jubilant Ivan Lendl wins his first Open crown.

LEFT: For the most part, John McEnroe let his racket do the talking in the finals against Ivan Lendl. But Lendl prevailed and beat McEnroe in straight sets 7–6, 6–3, 6–4.

BELOW: 1985 Wimbledon champion Boris Becker fell in the round of sixteen to Joakim Nystrom.

ABOVE & RIGHT: Hana
Mandlikova.

LEFT & BELOW: Hana
Mandlikova.

112

ping Claudia Kohde-Kilsch in the quarters, she gave Mandlikova every indication that she would be the finalist once more. She worked hard, but Mandlikova was too much. Hana took the semifinals 4–6, 6–2, 6–2.

In the women's final, Mandlikova withstood the heat (115 degrees at courtside), the sudden drop in temperature (to 80), the humidity (80 percent), and defending champion Navratilova. Mandlikova leaped to a 5–0 lead against Navratilova. Martina charged back for a 5–5 tie in the first set and, in a thrilling tiebreaker, the younger Czech player pounded home a crosscourt forehand winner, a service winner, a pure ace, and a low volley to take the tiebreaker 7–3.

After Navratilova powered her way through an overwhelmingly successful second set to tie a one set-all, Mandlikova held uniformly until presented with the right opportunity. She led 4–3 in the third set. When Navratilova began to serve little did she know that the contender was about to take calculated gambles, volley well, break and go ahead 5–3. But the defending champion, determined as ever, scored on two backhands that were above reproach, broke back, and then held serve for a 5–5 deadlock. Two games later the contenders were in a decisive tiebreaker.

Starting swiftly, Mandlikova pounced on Navratilova for a 6–0 lead in the tiebreaker. She took chances but played smart, as she turned in service winners, crosscourt winners, and other strong shots that caused errors. Navratilova caused her younger adversary to send one shot down the sideline and another over the baseline. That made it 6–2 and the crowd sensed a comeback by the defending champion. It was a false alarm.

Throughout the match and especially in the late stages of the battle, the crowd was very vocal for Mandlikova. "Hana! Hana!" they yelled.

The 1985 U.S. open was Hana's showcase. With this important victory, she served notice that she had arrived and that she had come to stay. In the final two rounds, she had overcome the game's top two players, and she beat both the same way, by serving better and volleying better but not as anxiously as in the past.

Her triumph brought into sharper focus her ascension to the top and her quest to surpass the older champions. "I think I'm at their level," said Mandlikova. "I think I'm playing as well as they do. They're older, more experienced, but I think I'm as good now."

In the men's doubles championship Ken Flach and Robert Seguso defeated France's Henri Leconte and Yannick Noah 6–7, 7–6, 7–6, 6–0. Claudia Kohde-Kilsch and Helena Sukova downed Navratilova and Shriver 6–7, 6–2, 6–3 in the women's title match. Navratilova teamed well with Heinz Gunthardt to topple Australia's Elizabeth Smylie (formerly Sayers) and John Fitzgerald 6–3, 6–3 to take top plaudits in the mixed doubles competition.

"The 1985 US Open was Hana's showcase."

114

"1986: Czech . . . Mate":

For the fifth consecutive year, *she* earned more than a million dollars. For the fifth straight year, *he* entered the U.S. Open finals with a great chance to be a champion. *Her* opponent was 21 years old, from the same native country as the champion. *His* opponent stood 6-foot-3 and weighed 180 pounds. Headed full speed towards the net, he was an imposing sight.

Who were *they?* In what country were *they* born? The answer is easy—Martina Navratilova (now officially a U.S. citizen), Ivan Lendl, Helena Sukova, Miloslav Mecir were the players, and they were all originally from Czechoslovakia. Their achievements may have looked easy, but looks can be deceptive. Their talent made it more than a matter of chance that their appearance in the finals marked the first time that four foreign-born players from the same country (Czechoslovakia) played in the men's and women's finals.

This event marked the first time since 1966 that no Americans appeared in the men's semifinals. Only Evert's appearance, her 16th, gave the United States representation in the quarterfinals.

The singles winners won $210,000 each, a record, and the tournament's purse had grown to an all-time high of $3,450,800.

A stirring skirmish in the semifinals between West German Steffi Graf, 17, and Navratilova brought attention to the quickly ascending Graf, involved in the tournament's most exciting match for the second straight year. Graf battled Navratilova to the wire, and each player had three match points before Navratilova reigned.

Navratilova had led the game early against Graf, 4–1, 15–30, until heavy rains, which flooded center court, had required suspending the game until the following day, Saturday. The top-seeded player rebounded to hold serve once the action resumed and proceeded to take the first set 6–1. Graf, however, broke early, held serve (spotlighted by a stinging ace) and shot ahead 2–0 in the second set. Navratilova had come back to go ahead 4–3 before Graf held serve with four straight points and broke the other player's serve for a 5–4 edge. Trailing 30–0 with Graf serving for the set, Navratilova took four points in a row to make it 5–5. Up 40–love, Navratilova committed five costly mistakes and the 11th game belonged to the young contender.

One more break and the set was tied 6–6. Tiebreaker in effect, Graf came up with a 7–3 edge by collecting three triumphant forehands, one winning backhand, an error by Martina, and two stinging aces. Graf had taken the set, 7–6.

The champion broke the challenger in the first game, set three, but Graf recovered with a break of her own in the eighth game. Graf, up 4–5, had two match points against Martina's serve, but saw two shots—a forehand and a service return—go long.

Battling their way into another suspenseful tiebreaker, Graf's third match point of the encounter ran awry and Navratilova failed her first chance to upend her opponent. At crucial times, Graf saw one backhand sail into the net, another carried over the baseline, and a third, facing Martina's match point, destruct after, to a sharply slicing serve from Martina. Navratilova took the honors, 6–1, 6–7, 7–6.

"She's a terrific player," praised Navratilova. "I hope she doesn't get much better; if she does, I'll quit."

TOP, LEFT: Ken Flach and Robert Seguso (near court) defeated Henri Leconte and Yannick Noah to take the U.S. Open men's doubles championship.

BOTTOM, LEFT: Helena Sukova and Claudia Kohde-Kilsch celebrate their first doubles win.

ABOVE: Yannick Noah.

Navratilova wanted another crown, but she would have to earn it over Helena Sukova, whose semifinals triumph over Evert was her first in 15 tries. The 6-foot-2 player had recorded one 1984 upset over Navratilova and wanted another.

Sukova bounded to a 3–1 lead in the first set. It was easy to see why she had made the finals: her serve-and-volley approach was working smoothly, and she had three service return winners in a row. Navratilova, however, unleashed her own attack, playing almost flawlessly at times to capture 11 of the next 13 points to win her third U.S. Open championship 6–3, 6–2.

"Helena looked shell-shocked out there," said Navratilova, after presenting her super-slamming, volley-winning, ultra-hustling style.

Navratilova left no doubts as to her ranking as the world's top women's tennis player. Conqueror of two French Opens, three Australian Opens, and seven Wimbledons, she now stood proudly, champion of three U.S. Opens.

"I know that I'm not a born American, but my heart is very much here," said Navratilova after winning. "This definitely has an extra edge on it because it is home."

The men's side of the ledger had changed when both Jimmy Connors and John McEnroe fell out after the first round of action. McEnroe lost almost everything—his confidence, his crispness, his serve, his zest—in the second set of the Open's second match. As a result, the four-time champion dropped his opening bid to Paul Annacone by 1–6, 6–1, 6–3, 6–3.

Stefan Edberg, the fourth seed who beat Tim Wilkison (6–3, 6–3, 6–3) at his own game in the quarterfinals, got nowhere with Lendl in the semifinals and lost 7–6, 6–2, 6–3 to the top seeded player.

Seeded 16 and the spoiler for Sweden's Joakim Nystrom (6–4, 6–2, 3–6, 6–2), Mecir conquered Becker, now all of 18 years of age, 4–6, 6–3, 6–4, 3–6, 6–3, to reach the finals.

Mecir had hoped to limit Lendl's championship record at the U.S. Open to one win, and he showed signs of surprising the fans when he broke Lendl in the second game after the defending champion had opened play with a break of his own. Having said in a press conference after seven days of play that he was "homesick" and desired "to go fishing" in the Czechoslovakian countryside, Mecir had parlayed a backhand volley and a forehand volley into an impressive ensemble, but at 3–3 Lendl took command.

Using his topspin forehands, Lendl rolled along with hardly a surprise. He won 6–4, 6–2, 6–0 over Mecir. Lendl was happy, expressing the emotions a finalist experiences after winning a title match. "It is hard to describe because for so long I didn't know how it feels to win the U.S. Open," he told the media. "Then I did it, and it felt good. Now, I do it again, and I want to do it next year."

"I have a funny way of looking at it," he also said, "You're working so hard to get to the finals of the majors, and when you get there, you're so nervous before the matches that you wish it were over. So in a way, I'm kind of laughing at myself, and saying, 'See, you bum, you're working so hard to get there and now you're there, you're worried.' And it's just more enjoyable that way."

ABOVE: Steffi Graf's rifle
forehand carried her to the
semifinals.

ABOVE, CENTER: Helena
Sukova's powerful serve
vaulted her into the finals
against Martina Navratilova.

ABOVE, RIGHT: Navratilova's
command of the net
brought her yet another
U.S. Open title.

ABOVE: Miloslav Mecir, who confessed to being homesick, defeated Boris Becker in the semifinals. His long reach and finesse enabled him to get to the finals where he lost to Ivan Lendl in straight sets.

ABOVE: Mikael Pernfors, another Swede on the horizon.

BELOW: Joakim Nystrom.

BELOW: Gabriela Sabatini.

BELOW: Tim Mayotte.

BELOW: Miloslav Mecir.

OVERLEAF, LEFT & BE-
LOW: Ivan Lendl's power,
speed and concentration
help him capture his sec-
ond U.S. Open title.

Such are the feelings of a U.S. Open champion. Becker and the Swedish players were on the horizon, but for now, the most prized laurels belonged to Lendl, who left no doubts as to his superiority.

In men's doubles, Andres Gomez and Slobodan Zivojinovic became champions by defeating Joakim Nystrom and Mats Wilander 4–6, 6–3, 6–3, 4–6, 6–3. Shriver and Navratilova won the women's doubles titles for the third time as a team when they edged Mandlikova and Turnbull 6–4, 3–6, 6–3. Raffaella Reggi and Sergio Casal downed Peter Fleming and Navratilova 6–4, 6–4 to command the top spot in the mixed doubles game.

6

Celebrities In The Stands

LEFT: Yoko Ono and Sean
Lennon

RIGHT: Bill Cosby

127

Johnny Carson

Kirk Douglas

Henry Kissinger

TOP, LEFT: Mike Wallace

BOTTOM, LEFT: Linda Evans

7

1987: A 10th Anniversary

1987—The U.S. Open's tenth anniversary in the National Tennis Center at Flushing Meadows. The bright stars that make the U.S. Open one of the most challenging competitions in the world. The special New York ambience. Celebrities in the crowd and celebration in the air. Nostalgia for an era as three of the world's top players—Connors, Evert, and McEnroe—shared the limelight. And finally, Martina Navratilova and Ivan Lendl, players with stamina and absolute commitment to the game.

As the Czechoslovakian-born tennis stars took center stage in the U.S. Open's 10th anniversary at the National Tennis Center, the experts said the competition was tougher than ever. West German Steffi Graf, all of 18, was ranked number one in the world. She had lost one match all year, the Wimbledon final—to Martina. The fans thought the time had arrived for Graf to take her turn as reigning queen. But Navratilova's era had not ended yet. Nor had Lendl's. Already a winner of the 1985 and 1986 U.S. Open tournaments, Lendl was facing serious competition by two eager and talented Swedish players, Stefan Edberg and Mats Wilander.

Earlier play set the tone for this tough year. Shooting for her seventh U.S. Open title, Chris Evert became the first woman to win 1,200 pro matches when she bumped off Brazil's Niege Dias 6–0, 6–1 in the second round. A few days later, though, she fell to Lori McNeil by a 3–6, 6–2, 6–4 count in the quarterfinals. Starting at age 16, Evert had reached the Open's semifinals 16 times straight. "I didn't have control over any of my shots," she said later. "I guess that happens when you get older. You have a few more bad days. And today was a bad day."

A loss for Chris Evert brought Lori McNeil's dream of success closer to reality. McNeil's hopes for future tennis stardom gave her words determination. "I'll attack the net at every opportunity," she said before meeting Graf in the semifinals. She did, too, 93 times.

In the second set of the semifinals, McNeil missed a sure winner of a slam at the net that would have broken Graf and made it 4–3 for the challenger. "I'll never forget that one," said McNeil. "I took my eye off the ball." The serve and volley specialist came within inches of becoming the first black woman to reach the U.S. Open finals since the Open era began in 1968. However, having defeated Pam Shriver in the quarterfinals 6–4, 6–3 (and thereby ending the fifth seeded player's 19-match winning streak), Graf upended McNeil 4–6, 6–2, 6–4.

Navratilova arrived at the semifinals insisting that any reference to her age as a factor in her play was "premature." She had already overwhelmed Lisa Bonder 6–2, 6–1 early in the classic for her 30th win in her

LEFT: Lori McNeil, a serve and volley specialist, defeated Chris Evert in the quarterfinals before losing to Steffi Graf in the semifinals.

133

"You don't like to give Connors any winning chances. He creates enough for himself."

LEFT: Zina Garrison.

BELOW: Helena Sukova.

last 31 Open singles matches. In the semifinals she took on Helena Sukova, who became a 6–2, 6–2 semifinal victim of the defending women's champion in 53 minutes. Martina made good on 67 percent of her first serves.

Martina Navratilova entered her fifth straight U.S. Open final with a 6–3 lifetime edge over Graf, who stood 61–1 on the 1987 year. The pair battled strength against strength, Graf's overwhelming forehand countering Martina's overheads and net play, until the match stood 6–6, first set. At 3–3 in the tiebreak, the young contender saw a backhand passing shot and a long forehand both miss their marks and, at 5–4, she missed another backhand passer as Martina charged the net. Then Navratilova closed out the set with a service winner.

Uniting crosscourt forehand winners and a strong service game, Navratilova took the second set, 6–1, and captured her fourth U.S. Open championship in six appearances in the finals. Battling the flu, Graf committed 31 unforced errors to the champion's 13. Martina approached the net 61 times, winning 35 points there.

"They say I had a bad year," said Navratilova. "But I'd like to have a bad year like this every year. I knew I could win; I just had to concentrate. I knew she was vulnerable on her backhand and when she crowds it, she's vulnerable on her forehand."

Like Chris Evert, John McEnroe found himself subdued in the quarterfinals. Seeded eighth and seeking his fifth U.S. Open title, he downed Slobodan Zivojinovic of Yugoslavia in five sets, but then found his magic missing against Lendl, in a quarterfinal round that ended 6–3, 6–3, 6–4. The powerful righthander's lobs overwhelmed him and he commented, "Lendl is just more into the sport than I am. This is his whole life. He's the same person on and off the court."

Celebrating his 35th birthday during the tournament's first week, Jimmy Connors enjoyed himself in the early rounds, "playing good tennis" and dispatching his opponents with ease. Champion in 1982 and 1983 over Lendl, Connors had more than hinted that the Czechoslovakian native choked on the big ones, so it was up to him to challenge Lendl in the semifinals. He had already eliminated Gilbert 4–6, 6–3, 6–4, 6–0 in the quarters. In this semifinal meeting, Lendl put on a pure clinic by rifling forehands precisely past Connors, taking the match in straight sets, 6–4, 6–2, 6–2. Although Connors returned serve as well as ever, he was no match for Lendl's incredible forehand power. Connors committed 39 unforced errors. He still went out a classy player. "I like short matches," said Lendl. "You don't like to give Connors any winning chances. He creates enough for himself."

The Swedish players Stefan Edberg and Mats Wilander met in the semifinal opposite Connors and Lendl. Edberg stood 2–0 in his last two encounters with his countryman, and he stood 58–9 on the year and 14–4 at the Open the last five years. "I feel good and I am playing well," he said. "Everything seems to be going the right way now. Maybe I can take advantage of it." He couldn't.

Wilander leaped to a 3–0 first set lead and won the first set 6–4. He went on to lose the second set 3–6. The match's key game was an 18-minute, 28-point third set battle which featured 11 deuces between a serve-and-volley man (Edberg) and his normally baseline-conscious opponent,

137

TOP, LEFT: Steffi Graf.

TOP, RIGHT: Martina Navratilova.

ABOVE: The powerful combination of Martina Navratilova and Pam Shriver took the women's doubles finals over Kathy Jordan and Elizabeth Smylie.

who was successfully mixing in his own uncharacteristic charges to the net. Wilander won the tussle and eventually the match, 6–4, 3–6, 6–3, 6–4.

With quickness as his most indisputable forte, Wilander became the first Swede to reach the Open's championship round since Borg in 1981. Wilander had lost to Lendl 6–2, 6–2, 6–2 in the fourth round of the 1982 U.S. Open, and Lendl had mastered him again in the 1983 quarters by 6–4, 6–4, 7–6.

The marathon finals match lasted four hours and 47 minutes, a finals record. Sick with the flu, Lendl commented "If it had been any other tournament, I wouldn't have played on Saturday [in the semis] and I wouldn't have played today [Monday, after rain washed out Sunday's scheduled finals play]. "I was out of juice the last three and a half sets. What got me through was strength of mind and a little bit of luck."

Down 5–6, 15–40 in the third set, Lendl reached back for something extra. On a day when he was "tired, dizzy, heavy, and slow," the title-holder boomed two big serves (an ace, and one that set up a narrow volley touch-winner) for deuce. Two more winners later, he was into the tie-breaker and had a 4–0 lead before Wilander bounced back to close on Lendl's lead to 5–4. His serve returned, the champion smashed an ace to take the set at 7–4. The deadlock had been resolved.

"Ivan is just more steady than anyone else. If I don't play well the whole match, he plays the same and wins."

At 4–5 and trying to go 5–5 in the fourth set, with Wilander serving, Lendl fused three superior returns into winners. The crown was once again his. He could claim 59 placement winners, 13 service aces, and 55 points won at the net (in 777 approaches) "If someone had told me three years ago that I would win this tournament [three years in a row], I would have thought they were crazy," he said. "I am very happy."

Wilander generously commented on Lendl's play. "Ivan is just more steady than anyone else. If I don't play well the whole match, he plays the same and wins."

In the intense men's doubles, Edberg had linked up with countryman Anders Jarryd to win the men's doubles by a 7–6, 6–2, 4–6, 5–7, 7–6 margin over Ken Flach and Robert Seguso. In the women's, the powerful combination of Navratilova and Pam Shriver took the women's doubles title 5–7, 6–4, 6–2 over Kathy Jordan and Elizabeth Smylie. Navratilova then joined forces with Emilio Sanchez to edge Betsy Nagelsen and Paul Annacone for a 6–4, 6–7, 7–6 mixed doubles championship. For becoming the tournament's first triple winner since Margaret Court in 1970, Navratilova collected $306,413.50. Lendl's $250,000 check put him well over $11 million in total lifetime tennis earnings.

RIGHT: Ivan Lendl.

ABOVE, LEFT: Mats Wilander makes his first appearance in the finals.

ABOVE, RIGHT: Stefan Edberg.

RIGHT: Thirty-five year-old Jimmy Connors makes another appearance in the U.S. Open semifinals.

Guillermo Vilas

CHAPTER 8 *The Struggles, or Masters of The Game*

Vince Lombardi, who became the high priest of competition, once said: "I will demand a commitment to excellence and to victory, and that is what life is all about." George Allen, former coach of the Washington Redskins, put it another way: "Every time you win, you're reborn; when you lose, you die a little."

One of the finest aspects of any sport, whether it be sandlot basketball or professional tennis, is the personal depletion the participants feel at the end of the game. It is the exhaustion that leads to the re-creation and the ultimate mastery of one's body and the mastery of the sport itself.

Getting to the top is the ultimate challenge for gifted players of any sport, and the road there is merely the prelude. The closer one gets, the sweeter the fruit. And the fruit can become an intoxicant.

The Olympic motto, "Faster, higher, and stronger," applies to today's tennis champions. The road they have traveled to be number one has been not so much for the destination as for the journey. In this journey, muscles, mind, spirit, and sacrifice come together to create a poetic grace of movement and response.

Bjorn Borg's obsession with winning the U.S. Open pushed him for more than eight years.

Billie Jean King, who returned to competition after knee surgery in 1977, said, "After all, tennis is my life, my art. I love to play the game. Staying on top is tough, but there's nothing else in the world like it. That's why we all keep coming back for more."

On the following pages, you will see some of the best players in the world—masters of the game. Some have already made it to the top. Others may be on their way. For each, the journey must begin somewhere.

Mats Wilander

Ivan Lendl

Hana Mandlikova

Martina Navratilova

Zina Garrison

Steffi Graf

Eliot Teltscher

Boris Becker

Pam Shriver

Virginia Wade

John McEnroe

Stefan Edberg

US Open Prize Money 1968–1987

YEAR & PRIZE MONEY	SINGLES		DOUBLES (per team)		MIXED DOUBLES (per team)
	Men	Women	Men	Women	
1968 — $100,000	$14,000	$6,000	$4,200	$1,750	No Money Awarded
1969 — $125,000	$16,000	$6,000	$3,000	$2,000	$2,000
1970 — $176,000	$20,000	$7,500	$3,000	$2,000	$2,000
1971 — $160,000	$15,000	$5,000	$2,000	$1,000	$1,000
1972 — $160,000	$25,000	$10,000	$3,000	$2,000	$2,000
1973 — $227,000	$25,000	$25,000	$4,000	$4,000	$2,000
1974 — $271,720	$22,500	$22,500	$4,500	$4,500	$2,000
1975 — $309,430	$25,000	$25,000	$4,500	$4,500	$2,000
1976 — $416,600	$30,000	$30,000	$10,000	$10,000	$6,500
1977 — $462,420	$33,000	$33,000	$13,125	$13,125	$6,500
1978 — $552,480	$38,000	$38,000	$15,500	$15,500	$6,500
1979 — $563,600	$39,000	$39,000	$15,750	$15,750	$7,100
1980 — $654,082	$46,000	$46,000	$18,500	$18,500	$7,100
1981 — $964,700	$66,000	$66,000	$26,400	$26,400	$9,680
1982 — $1,466,000	$90,000	$90,000	$36,000	$36,000	$14,000
1983 — $1,941,000	$120,000	$120,000	$48,000	$48,000	$17,000
1984 — $2,497,686	$160,000	$160,000	$64,000	$64,000	$17,000
1985 — $2,953,500	$187,500	$187,500	$65,000	$65,000	$19,000
1986 — $3,315,800	$210,000	$210,000	$72,800	$72,800	$21,800
1987 — $3,979,294	$250,000	$250,000	$86,667	$86,667	$26,160

National Men's Singles Finals, 1881–1987

Year	Champion	Rt/Lft Handed	Runner-up	Score
1881	Richard D. Sears	Right	W.E. Glyn	60 63 62
1882	Richard D. Sears	Right	Clarence M. Clark	61 64 60
1883	Richard D. Sears	Right	James Dwight	62 60 97
1884	Richard D. Sears	Right	Howard A. Taylor	60 16 60 62
1885	Richard D. Sears	Right	Godfrey M. Brinley	63 46 60 63
1886	Richard D. Sears	Right	R. Livingston Beeckman	46 61 63 64
1887	Richard D. Sears	Right	Henry W. Slocum, Jr.	61 63 62
1888*	Henry W. Slocum, Jr.	Right	Howard A. Taylor	64 61 60
1889	Henry W. Slocum, Jr.	Right	Q.A. Shaw	63 61 46 62
1890	Oliver S. Campbell	Right	Henry W. Slocum, Jr.	62 46 63 61
1891	Oliver S. Campbell	Right	Clarence Hobart	26 75 79 61 62
1892	Oliver S. Campbell	Right	Fred H. Hovey	75 36 63 75
1893*	Robert D. Wrenn	Left	Fred H. Hovey	64 36 64 64
1894	Robert D. Wrenn	Left	M.F. Goodbody	68 61 64 64
1895	Fred H. Hovey	Right	Robert D. Wrenn	63 62 64
1896	Robert D. Wrenn	Left	Fred H. Hovey	75 36 60 16 61
1897	Robert D. Wrenn	Left	W.V. Eaves	46 86 63 26 62
1898*	Malcolm D. Whitman	Right	Dwight F. Davis	36 62 62 61
1899	Malcolm D. Whitman	Right	J. Parmly Paret	61 62 36 75
1900	Malcolm D. Whitman	Right	William A. Larned	64 16 62 62
1901	William A. Larned	Right	Beals C. Wright	62 68 64 64
1902	William A. Larned	Right	Reginald F. Doherty	46 62 64 86
1903	Hugh L. Doherty	Right	William A. Larned	60 63 108
1904*	Holcombe Ward	Right	William J. Clothier	108 64 97
1905	Beals C. Wright	Left	Holcombe Ward	62 61 119
1906	William J. Clothier	Right	Beals C. Wright	63 60 64
1907*	William A. Larned	Right	Robert LeRoy	62 62 64
1908	William A. Larned	Right	Beals C. Wright	61 62 86
1909	William A. Larned	Right	William J. Clothier	61 62 57 16 61
1910	William A. Larned	Right	Thomas C. Bundy	61 57 60 68 61
1911	William A. Larned	Right	Maurice E. McLoughlin	64 64 62
1912†	Maurice E. McLoughlin	Right	Wallace F. Johnson	36 26 62 64 62
1913	Maurice E. McLoughlin	Right	Richard N. Williams	64 57 63 61
1914	Richard N. Williams	Right	Maurice E. McLoughlin	63 86 108
1915	William M. Johnston	Right	Maurice E. McLoughlin	16 60 75 108
1916	Richard N. Williams	Right	William M. Johnston	46 64 06 62 64
1917	R. Lindley Murray	Left	N.W. Niles	57 86 63 63
1918	R. Lindley Murray	Left	William T. Tilden	63 61 75
1919	William M. Johnston	Right	William T. Tilden	64 64 63
1920	William T. Tilden	Right	William M. Johnston	61 16 75 57 63
1921	William T. Tilden	Right	Wallace J. Johnson	61 63 61
1922	William T. Tilden	Right	William M. Johnston	46 36 62 63 64
1923	William T. Tilden	Right	William M. Johnston	64 61 64
1924	William T. Tilden	Right	William M. Johnston	61 97 62
1925	William T. Tilden	Right	William M. Johnston	46 119 63 46 63
1926	Rene Lacoste	Right	Jean Borotra	64 60 64
1927	Rene Lacoste	Right	William T. Tilden	119 63 119
1928	Henri Cochet	Right	Francis T. Hunter	46 64 36 75 63
1929	William T. Tilden	Right	Francis T. Hunter	36 63 46 62 64
1930	John H. Doeg	Left	Francis X. Shields	108 16 64 1614
1931	H. Ellsworth Vines	Right	George M. Lott, Jr.	79 63 97 75
1932	H. Ellsworth Vines	Right	Henri Cochet	64 64 64
1933	Frederick J. Perry	Right	John H. Crawford	63 1113 46 60 61
1934	Frederick J. Perry	Right	Wilmer L. Allison	64 63 16 86
1935	Wilmer L. Allison	Right	Sidney B. Wood	62 62 63
1936	Fred Perry	Right	J. Donald Budge	26 62 86 16 108
1937	J. Donald Budge	Right	Baron Gottfried von Cramm	61 79 61 36 61
1938	J. Donald Budge	Right	C. Gene Mako	63 68 62 61
1939	Robert Riggs	Right	S. Welby van Horn	64 62 64
1940	Donald McNeill	Right	Robert Riggs	46 68 63 63 75
1941	Robert Riggs	Right	Francis Kovacs, 2d	63 61 63
1942	Frederick R. Schroeder, Jr.	Right	Frank Parker	86 75 36 46 62
1943	Lt. Joseph R. Hunt	Right	Seaman John A. Kramer	63 68 108 60
1944	Sgt. Frank Parker	Right	William F. Talbert	64 36 63 63
1945	Sgt. Frank Parker	Right	William F. Talbert	1412 61 62
1946	John A. Kramer	Right	Tom Brown, Jr.	97 63 60
1947	John A. Kramer	Right	Frank Parker	46 26 61 60 63
1948	Richard A. Gonzales	Right	Eric W. Sturgess	62 63 1412
1949	Richard A. Gonzales	Right	Frederick Schroeder	1618 26 61 62 64
1950	Arthur Larsen	Left	Herbert Flam	63 46 57 64 63
1951	Frank Sedgman	Right	E. Victor Seixas, Jr.	64 61 61
1952	Frank Sedgman	Right	Gardnar Mulloy	61 62 63
1953	Tony Trabert	Right	E. Victor Seixas, Jr.	63 62 63
1954	E. Victor Seixas, Jr.	Right	Rex Hartwig	36 62 64 64
1955	Tony Trabert	Right	Ken Rosewall	97 63 63
1956	Ken Rosewall	Right	Lewis Hoad	46 62 63 63
1957	Malcolm J. Anderson	Right	Ashley J. Cooper	108 75 64
1958	Ashley J. Cooper	Right	Malcolm J. Anderson	62 36 46 108 86
1959	Neale Fraser	Left	Alejandro Olmedo	63 57 62 64
1960	Neale Fraser	Left	Rodney Laver	64 64 97
1961	Roy Emerson	Right	Rodney Laver	75 63 62
1962	Rodney Laver	Left	Roy Emerson	62 64 57 64
1963	Rafael Osuna	Right	Frank Froehling, III	75 64 62
1964	Roy Emerson	Right	Fred Stolle	64 62 64
1965	Manuel Santana	Right	Cliff Drysdale	62 79 75 61
1966	Fred Stolle	Right	John Newcombe	46 1210 63 64
1967	John Newcombe	Right	Clark Graebner	64 64 86

Open Champions— Men's Singles

Year	Champion	Rt/Lft Handed	Runner-up	Score
1968	Arthur Ashe	Right	Tom Okker	1412 57 63 36 63
1969	Rod Laver	Left	Tony Roche	79 61 62 62
1970	Ken Rosewall	Right	Tony Roche	26 64 76 63
1971	Stan Smith	Right	Jan Kodes	36 63 62 76
1972	Ilie Nastase	Right	Arthur Ashe	36 63 67 64 63
1973	John Newcombe	Right	Jan Kodes	64 16 46 62 62
1974	Jimmy Connors	Left	Ken Rosewall	61 60 61
1975	Manuel Orantes	Left	Jimmy Connors	64 63 63
1976	Jimmy Connors	Left	Bjorn Borg	64 36 76 64
1977	Guillermo Vilas	Left	Jimmy Connors	26 63 75 60
1978	Jimmy Connors	Left	Bjorn Borg	64 62 62
1979	John McEnroe	Left	Vitas Gerulaitis	75 63 63
1980	John McEnroe	Left	Bjorn Borg	76 61 67 57 64
1981	John McEnroe	Left	Bjorn Borg	46 62 64 63
1982	Jimmy Connors	Left	Ivan Lendl	63 62 46 64
1983	Jimmy Connors	Left	Ivan Lendl	63 67 75 60
1984	John McEnroe	Left	Ivan Lendl	63 64 61
1985	Ivan Lendl	Right	John McEnroe	76 63 64
1986	Ivan Lendl	Right	Miloslav Mecir	64 62 60
1987	Ivan Lendl	Right	Mats Wilander	67 60 76 64

Year	Champion	Rt/Lft Handed	Runner-up	Score
1887	Ellen Hansell	Right	Laura Knight	61 60
1888	Bertha L. Townsend	Right	Ellen Hansell	63 65
1889	Bertha L. Townsend	Right	Louise D. Voorhees	75 62
1890	Ellen C. Roosevelt	Right	Bertha L. Townsend	62 62
1891	Mabel Cahill	Right	Ellen C. Roosevelt	64 61 46 63
1892	Mabel Cahill	Right	Elisabeth Moore	57 63 64 46 62
1893*	Aline Terry	Right	Alice Schultz	61 63
1894	Helen Hellwig	Right	Aline Terry	75 36 60 36 63
1895	Juliette Atkinson	Right	Helen Hellwig	64 62 61
1896	Elisabeth Moore	Right	Juliette Atkinson	64 46 62 62
1897	Juliette Atkinson	Right	Elisabeth Moore	63 63 46 36 63
1898	Juliette Atkinson	Right	Marion Jones	63 57 64 26 75
1899*	Marion Jones	Right	Maud Banks	61 61 75
1900*	Myrtle McAteer	Right	Edith Parker	62 62 60
1901	Elisabeth Moore	Right	Myrtle McAteer	64 36 75 26 62
1902	Marion Jones	Right	Elisabeth Moore	61 10 ret.
1903	Elisabeth Moore	Right	Marion Jones	75 86
1904	May Sutton	Right	Elisabeth Moore	61 62
1905*	Elisabeth Moore	Right	Helen Homans	64 57 61
1906*	Helen Homans	Right	Maud Barger-Wallach	64 63
1907*	Evelyn Sears	Left	Carrie Neely	63 62
1908	Maud Barger-Wallach	Right	Evelyn Sears	63 16 63
1909	Hazel Hotchkiss	Right	Maud Barger-Wallach	60 61
1910	Hazel Hotchkiss	Right	Louise Hammond	64 62
1911	Hazel Hotchkiss	Right	Florence Sutton	810 61 97
1912*	Mary K. Browne	Right	Eleonora Sears	64 62
1913	Mary K. Browne	Right	Dorothy Green	62 75
1914	Mary K. Browne	Right	Marie Wagner	62 16 61
1915*	Molla Bjurstedt	Right	Hazel Hotchkiss Wightman	46 62 60
1916	Molla Bjurstedt	Right	Louise Hammond Raymond	60 61
1917*	Molla Bjurstedt	Right	Marion Vanderhoef	46 60 62
1918	Molla Bjurstedt	Right	Eleanor E. Goss	64 63
1919†	Hazel H. Wightman	Right	Marion Zinderstein	61 62
1920	Molla B. Mallory	Right	Marion Zinderstein	63 61
1921	Molla B. Mallory	Right	Mary K. Browne	46 64 62
1922	Molla B. Mallory	Right	Helen Wills	63 61
1923	Helen Wills	Right	Molla B. Mallory	62 61
1924	Helen Wills	Right	Molla B. Mallory	61 63
1925	Helen Wills	Right	Kathleen McKane	36 60 62
1926	Molla B. Mallory	Right	Elizabeth Ryan	46 64 97
1927	Helen Wills	Right	Betty Nuthall	61 64
1928	Helen Wills	Right	Helen H. Jacobs	62 61
1929	Helen Wills	Right	Phoebe Holcroft Watson	64 62
1930	Betty Nuthall	Right	Anna McCune Harper	61 64
1931	Helen Wills Moody	Right	Eileen Bennett Whitingstall	64 61
1932	Helen H. Jacobs	Right	Carolin A. Babcock	62 62
1933	Helen H. Jacobs	Right	Helen Wills Moody	86 36 30 ret.
1934	Helen H. Jacobs	Right	Sarah H. Palfrey	61 64
1935	Helen H. Jacobs	Right	Sarah Palfrey Fabyan	62 64
1936	Alice Marble	Right	Helen H. Jacobs	46 63 62
1937	Anita Lizana	Right	Jadwiga Jedrzejowska	64 62
1938	Alice Marble	Right	Nancye Wynne	60 63
1939	Alice Marble	Right	Helen H. Jacobs	60 810 64
1940	Alice Marble	Right	Helen H. Jacobs	62 63
1941	Sarah Palfrey Cooke	Right	Pauline Betz	75 62
1942	Pauline Betz	Right	A. Louise Brough	46 61 64
1943	Pauline Betz	Right	A. Louise Brough	63 57 63
1944	Pauline Betz	Right	Margaret Osborne	63 86
1945	Sarah Palfrey Cooke	Right	Pauline Betz	36 86 64
1946	Pauline Betz	Right	Patricia Canning	119 63
1947	A. Louise Brough	Right	Margaret Osborne	86 46 61
1948	Margaret Osborne duPont	Right	A. Louise Brough	46 64 1513
1949	Margaret Osborne duPont	Right	Doris Hart	64 61
1950	Margaret Osborne duPont	Right	Doris Hart	63 63
1951	Maureen Connolly	Right	Shirley Fry	63 16 64
1952	Maureen Connolly	Right	Doris Hart	63 75
1953	Maureen Connolly	Right	Doris Hart	62 64
1954	Doris Hart	Right	A. Louise Brough	68 61 86
1955	Doris Hart	Right	Patricia Ward	64 62
1956	Shirley J. Fry	Right	Althea Gibson	63 64
1957	Althea Gibson	Right	A. Louise Brough	63 62
1958	Althea Gibson	Right	Darlene Hard	36 61 62
1959	Maria Bueno	Right	Christine Truman	61 64
1960	Darlene R. Hard	Right	Maria Bueno	64 1012 64
1961	Darlene R. Hard	Right	Ann Haydon	63 64
1962	Margaret Smith	Right	Darlene Hard	97 64
1963	Maria Bueno	Right	Margaret Smith	75 64
1964	Maria Bueno	Right	Carole Caldwell Graebner	61 60
1965	Margaret Smith	Right	Billie Jean Moffitt	86 75
1966	Maria Bueno	Right	Nancy Richey	63 61
1967	Billie Jean Moffitt King	Right	Ann Haydon Jones	119 64

Year	Champion	Rt/Lft Handed	Runner-up	Score
1968	Virginia Wade	Right	Billie Jean King	64 64
1969	Margaret Smith Court	Right	Nancy Richey	62 62
1970	Margaret Smith Court	Right	Rosemary Casals	62 26 61
1971	Billie Jean King	Right	Rosemary Casals	64 76
1972	Billie Jean King	Right	Kerry Melville	63 75
1973	Margaret Smith Court	Right	Evonne Goolagong	76 57 62
1974	Billie Jean King	Right	Evonne Goolagong	36 63 75
1975	Christine Marie Evert	Right	Evonne Goolagong	57 64 62
1976	Christine Marie Evert	Right	Evonne Goolagong	63 60
1977	Christine Marie Evert	Right	Wendy Turnbull	76 62
1978	Christine Marie Evert	Right	Pamela Shriver	75 64
1979	Tracy Austin	Right	Chris Evert Lloyd	64 63
1980	Chris Evert Lloyd	Right	Hana Mandlikova	57 61 61
1981	Tracy Austin	Right	Martina Navratilova	16 76 76
1982	Chris Evert Lloyd	Right	Hana Mandlikova	63 61
1983	Martina Navratilova	Left	Chris Evert Lloyd	61 63
1984	Martina Navratilova	Left	Chris Evert Lloyd	46 64 64
1985	Hana Mandlikova	Right	Martina Navratilova	76 16 76
1986	Martina Navratilova	Left	Helena Sukova	63 62
1987	Martina Navratilova	Left	Steffi Graf	64 61

*No Challenge Round played
†Challenge Round abolished

Year	Champions	Runners-up	Score
1881	Clarence M. Clark - Fred W. Taylor	Alexander Van Rensselaer - A.E. Newbold	65 64 65
1882	Richard D. Sears - James Dwight	W. Nightingale - G.M. Smith	62 64 64
1883	Richard D. Sears - James Dwight	Alexander Van Rensselaer - A.E. Newbold	60 62 62
1884	Richard D. Sears - James Dwight	Alexander Van Rensselaer - W.V.R. Berry	64 61 810 64
1885	Richard D. Sears - Joseph S. Clark	Henry W. Slocum, Jr. - W.P. Knapp	63 60 62
1886	Richard D. Sears - James Dwight	Howard A. Taylor - Godfrey M. Brinley	75 57 75 64
1887	Richard D. Sears - James Dwight	Howard A. Taylor - Henry W. Slocum, Jr.	64 36 26 63 63
1888	Oliver S. Campbell - Valentine G. Hall	Clarence Hobart - E.P. Macmullen	64 62 64
1889	Henry W. Slocum, Jr. - Howard A. Taylor	Valentine G. Hall - Oliver S. Campbell	61 63 62
1890	Valentine G. Hall - Clarence Hobart	Charles Carver - John Ryerson	63 46 62 26 63
1891	Oliver Campbell - Robert Huntington, Jr.	Valentine G. Hall - Clarence Hobart	63 64 86
1892	Oliver Campbell - Robert Huntington, Jr.	Valentine G. Hall - Edward L. Hall	64 62 46 63
1893	Clarence Hobart - Fred H. Hovey	Oliver Campbell - Robert Huntington, Jr.	63 64 46 62
1894	Clarence Hobart - Fred H. Hovey	Carr B. Neel - Samuel R. Neel	63 86 61
1895	Malcolm G. Chace - Robert D. Wrenn	Clarence Hobart - Fred Hovey	75 61 86
1896	Carr B. Neel - Samuel R. Neel	Robert D. Wrenn - Malcolm G. Chase	63 16 61 36 61
1897	Leo E. Ware - George P. Sheldon, Jr.	Harold S. Mahony - Harold A. Nisbet	1113 62 97 16 61
1898	Leo E. Ware - George P. Sheldon, Jr.	Holcombe Ward - Dwight F. Davis	16 75 64 46 75
1899	Holcombe Ward - Dwight F. Davis	Leo E. Ware - George P. Sheldon, Jr.	64 64 63
1900	Holcombe Ward - Dwight F. Davis	Fred B. Alexander - Raymond D. Little	64 97 1210
1901	Holcombe Ward - Dwight F. Davis	Leo E. Ware - Beals C. Wright	63 97 61
1902	Reginald F. Doherty - Hugh L. Doherty	Holcombe Ward - Dwight F. Davis	119 1210 64
1903	Reginald F. Doherty - Hugh L. Doherty	Kriegh Collins - L. Harry Waidner	75 63 63
1904	Holcombe Ward - Beals C. Wright	Kriegh Collins - Raymond D. Little	16 62 36 64 61
1905	Holcombe Ward - Beals C. Wright	Fred B. Alexander - Harold H. Hackett	64 64 61
1906	Holcombe Ward - Beals C. Wright	Fred B. Alexander - Harold H. Hackett	63 36 63 63
1907	Fred B. Alexander - Harold H. Hackett	Nat Thornton - B.M. Grant	62 61 61
1908	Fred B. Alexander - Harold H. Hackett	Raymond D. Little - Beals C. Wright	61 75 62
1909	Fred B. Alexander - Harold H. Hackett	Maurice E. McLoughlin - George J. Janes	64 64 60
1910	Fred B. Alexander - Harold H. Hackett	Thos. C. Bundy - Trowbridge W. Hendrick	61 86 63
1911	Raymond D. Little - Gustave Touchard	Fred B. Alexander - Harold H. Hackett	75 1315 62 64
1912	Maurice McLoughlin - Thomas Bundy	Raymond D. Little - Gustave F. Touchard	36 62 61 75
1913	Maurice McLoughlin - Thomas Bundy	John R. Strachan - Clarence J. Griffin	64 75 61
1914	Maurice McLoughlin - Thomas Bundy	George M. Church - Dean Mathey	64 62 64
1915	William Johnston - Clarence Griffin	Maurice E. McLoughlin - Thomas C. Bundy	26 63 64 36 63
1916	William Johnston - Clarence Griffin	Maurice E. McLoughlin - Ward Dawson	64 63 57 63
1917	Fred Alexander - Harold Throckmorton	Harry C. Johnson - Irving C. Wright	119 64 64
1918	William Tilden, 2nd - Vincent Richards	Fred B. Alexander - Beals C. Wright	63 64 36 26 62
1919	Norman E. Brookes - Gerald Patterson	William T. Tilden, 2nd - Vincent Richards	86 63 46 46 62
1920	William Johnston - Clarence Griffin	Willis F. Davis - Roland E. Roberts	62 62 63
1921	William Tilden, 2nd - Vincent Richards	R.N. Williams, 2nd - W.M. Washburn	1311 1210 61
1922	William Tilden, 2nd - Vincent Richards	Gerald L. Patterson - Pat O'Hara Wood	46 61 63 64
1923	William Tilden, 2nd - Brian I.C. Norton	R.N. Williams 2nd - W.M. Washburn	36 62 63 57 62
1924	Howard Kinsey - Robert Kinsey	Gerald L. Patterson - Pat O'Hara Wood	75 57 79 63 64
1925	R.N. Williams, 2nd - Vincent Richards	Gerald Patterson - John B. Hawkes	62 810 64 119
1926	R.N. Williams, 2nd - Vincent Richards	William T. Tilden, 2nd - Alfred H. Chapin, Jr.	64 68 119 63
1927	William Tilden, 2nd - Francis T. Hunter	W.M. Johnston - R.N. Williams, 2nd	108 63 63
1928	George M. Lott, Jr. - John Hennessey	Gerald L. Patterson - John B. Hawkes	62 61 62
1929	George M. Lott, Jr. - John H. Doeg	Berkeley Bell - Lewis N. White	108 1614 61
1930	George M. Lott, Jr. - John H. Doeg	John Van Ryn - Wilmer Allison	86 63 36 1315 64
1931	Wilmer Allison - John Van Ryn	Gregory Mangin - Berkeley Bell	64 63 62
1932	H. Ellsworth Vines, Jr. - Keith Gledhill	Wilmer L. Allison - John Van Ryn	64 63 62
1933	George M. Lott, Jr. - Lester R. Stoefen	Francis X. Shields - Frank A. Parker	1113 97 97 63
1934	George M. Lott, Jr. - Lester R. Stoefen	Wilmer L. Allison - John Van Ryn	64 97 36 64
1935	Wilmer L. Allison - John Van Ryn	J. Donald Budge - C. Gene Mako	62 63 26 36 61
1936	J. Donald Budge - C. Gene Mako	Wilmer L. Allison - John Van Ryn	64 62 64
1937	Gottfried von Cramm - Henner Henkel	J. Donald Budge - C. Gene Mako	64 75 64
1938	J. Donald Budge - C. Gene Mako	Adrian K. Quist - John Bromwich	63 62 61
1939	Adrian K. Quist - John E. Bromwich	John A. Crawford - Harry C. Hopman	86 61 64
1940	John Kramer - Frederick Schroeder, Jr.	Gardnar Mulloy - Henry J. Prussoff	64 86 97
1941	John Kramer - Frederick Schroeder, Jr.	Wayne Sabin - Gardnar Mulloy	97 64 62
1942	Lt. Gardner Mulloy - William Talbert	Frederick Schroeder, Jr. - Sidney B. Wood, Jr.	97 75 61
1943	John Krame - Frank A. Parker	William Talbert - David Freeman	62 64 64
1944	Lt. W. Donald McNeill - Robert Falkenburg	William Talbert - Francisco Segura	75 64 36 61
1945	Lt. Gardnar Mulloy - William Talbert	Robert Falkenbury - Jack Tuero	1210 810 1210 62
1946	Gardnar Mulloy - William Talbert	Donald McNeill - Frank Guernsey	36 64 26 63 2018
1947	John Kramer - Frederick Schroeder, Jr.	William Talbert - William Sidwell	64 75 63
1948	Gardnar Mulloy - William Talbert	Frank A. Parker - Frederick R. Schroeder, Jr.	16 97 63 36 97
1949	John Bromwich - William Sidwell	Frank Sedgman - George Worthington	64 60 61
1950	John Bromwich - Frank Sedgman	William Talbert - Gardnar Mulloy	75 86 36 61
1951	Kenneth McGregor - Frank Sedgman	Don Candy - Mervyn Rose	108 64 46 75
1952	Mervyn Rose - E. Victor Seixas, Jr.	Kenneth McGregor - Frank Sedgman	36 108 108 68 86
1953	Rex Hartwig - Mervyn Rose	Gardnar Mulloy - William F. Talbert	64 46 62 64
1954	E. Victor Seixas, Jr. - Tony Trabert	Lewis Hoad - Ken Rosewall	36 64 86 63
1955	Kosei Kamo - Atushi Miyagi	Gerald Moss - William Quillan	63 63 36 16 64
1956	Lewis Hoad - Kenneth Rosewall	Hamilton Richardson - E. Victor Seixas, Jr.	62 62 36 64
1957	Ashley J. Cooper - Neale Fraser	Gardnar Mulloy - Budge Patty	46 63 97 63
1958	Alex Olmedo - Hamilton Richardson	Sam Giammalva - Barry MacKay	36 63 64 64
1959	Neale Fraser - Roy Emerson	Alex Olmedo - Earl Buchholz, Jr.	36 63 57 64 75
1960	Neale Fraser - Roy Emerson	Rod Laver - Bob Mark	97 62 64
1961	Charles McKinley - Dennis Ralston	Rafael Osuna - Antonio Palafox	63 64 26 1311
1962	Rafael Osuna - Antonio Palafox	Charles McKinley - Dennis Ralston	62 1012 16 97 63
1963	Charley McKinley - Dennis Ralston	Rafael Osuna - Antonio Palafox	97 46 57 63 119
1964	Charles McKinley - Dennis Ralston	Graham Stilwell - Mile Sangster	63 62 64
1965	Roy Emerson - Fred Stolle	Frank Froehling, III - Charles Pasarell	64 1012 75 73
1966	Roy Emerson - Fred Stolle	Clark Graebner - Dennis Ralston	64 64 64
1967	John Newcombe - Tony Roche	William Bowrey - Owen Davidson	68 97 63 63

Year	Champions	Runners-up	Score
1968	Robert Lutz - Stan Smith	Arthur Ashe - Andres Gimeno	119 61 75
1969	Ken Rosewall - Fred Stolle	Charles Pasarell - Dennis Ralston	26 75 1311 63
1970	Pierre Barthes - Nicki Pilic	Roy Emerson - Rod Laver	63 76 46 76
1971	John Newcombe - Roger Taylor	Stan Smith - Erik van Dillen	67 63 76 46 76
1972	Cliff Drysdale - Roger Taylor	Owen Davidson - John Newcombe	64 76 63
1973	Owen Davidson - John Newcombe	Rod Laver - Ken Rosewall	75 26 75 75
1974	Robert Lutz - Stan Smith	Patricio Cornejo - Jaime Fillol	63 63
1975	Jimmy Connors - Ilie Nastase	Tom Okker - Martin Riessen	64 76
1976	Marty Riessen - Tom Okker	Paul Kronk - Cliff Letcher	64 64
1977	Bob Hewitt - Frew McMillan	Brian Gottfried - Raul Ramirez	64 60
1978	Robert Lutz - Stan Smith	Marty Riessen - Sherwood Stewart	16 75 63
1979	John McEnroe - Peter Fleming	Robert Lutz - Stan Smith	62 64
1980	Robert Lutz - Stan Smith	John McEnroe - Peter Fleming	76 36 61 36 63
1981	John McEnroe - Peter Fleming	Heinz Gunthardt - Peter McNamara	default
1982	Kevin Curren - Steve Denton	Victor Amaya - Hank Pfister	62 67 57 62 64
1983	John McEnroe - Peter Fleming	Fritz Buehning - Van Winitsky	63 64 62
1984	John Fitzgerald - Tomas Smid	Stefan Edberg - Anders Jarryd	76 63 63
1985	Ken Flach - Robert Seguso	Henri Leconte - Yannick Noah	67 76 76 60
1986	Andres Gomez - Slobodan Zivojinovic	Joakim Nystrom - Mats Wilander	46 63 63 46 63
1987	Stefan Edberg - Anders Jarryd	Ken Flach - Robert Seguso	76 62 46 56 76

Year	Champions	Runners-up	Score
1890	Ellen C. Roosevelt - Grace W. Roosevelt	Bertha L. Townsend - Margarette L. Ballard	61 62
1891	Mabel Cahill - Mrs. W. Fellowes Morgan	Grace Roosevelt - Ellen C. Roosevelt	26 86 64
1892	Mabel E. Cahill - A.M. McKinlay	Mrs. A.H. Harris - Amy R. Williams	61 63
1893	Aline M. Terry - Hattie Butler	Alice L. Schultz - Miss Stone	64 63
1894	Helen R. Hellwig - Juliette P. Atkinson	A.C. Wistar - Amy R. Williams	64 86 62
1895	Helen R. Hellwig - Juliette P. Atkinson	Elisabeth H. Moore - Amy R. Williams	62 62 1210
1896	Elisabeth H. Moore - Juliette P. Atkinson	A.C. Wistar - Amy R. Williams	64 75
1897	Juliette P. Atkinson - Kathleen Atkinson	Mrs. F. Edwards - Elizabeth J. Rastall	62 61 61
1898	Juliette P. Atkinson - Kathleen Atkinson	Marie Wimer - Carrie B. Neely	61 26 46 61 62
1899	Jane W. Craven - Myrtle McAteer	Maud Banks - Elizabeth J. Rastall	61 61 75
1900	Edith Parker - Hallie Champlin	Marie Wimer - Myrtle McAteer	97 62 62
1901	Juliette P. Atkinson - Myrtle McAteer	Marion Jones - Elisabeth H. Moore	default
1902	Juliette P. Atkinson - Marion Jones	Maud Banks - Nona Closterman	62 75
1903	Elisabeth H. Moore - Carrie B.. Neely	Miriam Hall - Marion Jones	64 61 61
1904	May G. Sutton - Miriam Hall	Elisabeth H. Moore - Carrie B. Neely	36 63 63
1905	Helen Homans - Carrie B. Neely	M.F. Oberteuffer - Virginia Maule	60 61
1906	Mrs. L.S. Coe - Mrs. D.S. Plat	Helen Homans - Clover Boldt	64 64
1907	Marie Weimer - Carrie B. Neely	Edna Wildey - Natalie Wildey	61 26 64
1908	Evelyn Sears - Margaret Curtis	Carrie B. Neely - Marion Steever	63 57 97
1909	Hazel V. Hotchkiss - Edith E. Rotch	Dorothy Green - Lois Moyes	61 61
1910	Hazel V. Hotchkiss - Edith E. Rotch	Adelaide Browning - Edna Wildey	64 64
1911	Hazel V. Hotchkiss - Eleanora Sears	Dorothy Green - Florence Sutton	64 46 62
1912	Dorothy Green - Mary K. Browne	Maud Barger - Wallach - Mrs. Frederick Schmitz	62 57 60
1913	Mary K. Browne - Mrs. R. H. Williams	Dorothy Green - Edna Wildey	1210 26 63
1914	Mary K. Browne - Mrs. R. H. Williams	Louise H. Raymond - Edna Wildey	86 62
1915	Hazel Hotchkiss Wightman - Eleonora Sears	Helen H. McLean - Mrs. G. L. Chapman	108 62
1916	Molla Bjurstedt - Eleanora Sears	Louise H. Raymond - Edna Wildey	46 62 108
1917	Molla Bjurstedt - Eleanora Sears	Phyllis Walsh - Mrs. Robet LeRoy	62 64
1918	Marion Zinderstein - Eleanor Goss	Molla Bjurstedt - Mrs. Johan Rogge	75 86
1919	Marion Zinderstein - Eleanor Goss	Eleanora Sears - Hazel H. Wightman	108 97
1920	Marion Zinderstein - Eleanor Goss	Eleanor Tennant - Helen Baker	63 61
1921	Mary K. Browne - Mrs. R. H. Williams	Helen Gilleaudeau - Mrs. L.G. Morris	63 62
1922	Marion Zinderstein Jessup - Helen N. Wills	Edith Sigourney - Molla B. Mallory	64 79 63
1923	Kathleen McKane - Phyllis H. Covell	Hazel H. Wightman - Eleanor Goss	26 62 61
1924	Hazel H. Wightman - Helen N. Wills	Eleanor Goss - Marion Z. Jessup	64 63
1925	Mary K. Browne - Helen N. Wills	May S. Bundy - Elizabeth Ryan	64 63
1926	Elizabeth Ryan - Eleanor Goss	Mary K. Browne - Charlotte H. Chapin	36 64 1210
1927	Kathleen Godfree - Ermyntrude Harvey	Betty Nuthall - Joan Fry	61 46 64
1928	Hazel H. Wightman - Helen N. Wills	Edith Cross - Anna McCune Harper	62 62
1929	Phoebe Watson - Peggy S. Michell	Phyllis Covel - Mrs. D.C. Shepherd - Barron	26 63 64
1930	Betty Nuthall - Sarah Palfrey	Edith Cross - Anna McCune Harper	36 63 75
1931	Betty Nuthall - Eileen B. Whitingstall	Helen Jacobs - Dorothy Round	62 64
1932	Helen Jacobs - Sarah Palfrey	Edith Cross - Anna McCune Harper	36 63 75
1933	Betty Nuthall - Freda James	Helen Wills Moody - Elizabeth Ryan	default
1934	Helen Jacobs - Sarah Palfrey	Carolin A. Babcock - Dorothy Andrus	46 63 64
1935	Helen Jacobs - Sarah Palfrey Fabyan	Carolin A. Babcock - Dorothy Andrus	64 62
1936	Marjorie G. VanRyn - Carolin Babcock	Helen Jacobs - Sarah Palfrey Fabyan	97 26 64
1937	Sarah Palfrey Fabyan - Alice Marble	Marjorie G. Van Ryn - Carolin Babcock	75 64
1938	Sarah Palfrey Fabyan - Alice Marble	Rene Mathieu - Jadwiga Jedrzejowska	68 64 63
1939	Sarah Palfrey Fabyan - Alice Marble	Kay Stammers - Freda Hammersley	75 86
1940	Sarah Palfrey Fabyan - Alice Marble	Dorothy Bundy - Marjorie G. Van Ryn	64 63
1941	Sarah P. Fabyan - Margaret Osborne	Dorothy Bundy - Pauline Betz	36 61 64
1942	A. Louise Brough - Margaret E. Osborne	Pauline Betz - Doris Hart	26 75 60
1943	A. Louise Brough - Margaret E. Osborne	Patricia C. Todd - Mary A. Prentiss	61 63
1944	A. Louise Brough - Margaret E. Osborne	Pauline Betz - Doris Hart	46 64 63
1945	A. Louise Brough - Margaret E. Osborne	Pauline Betz - Doris Hart	63 63
1946	A. Louise Brough - Margaret E. Osborne	Patricia C. Todd - Mary A. Prentiss	61 63
1947	A. Louise Brough - Margaret E. Osborne	Patricia C. Todd - Doris Hart	57 63 75
1948	A. Louise Brough - Margaret O. duPont	Patricia C. Todd - Doris Hart	64 810 61
1949	A. Louise Brough - Margaret O. duPont	Doris Hart - Shirley Fry	64 108
1950	A. Louise Brough - Margaret O. duPont	Doris Hart - Shirley Fry	62 63
1951	Shirley Fry - Doris Hart	Nancy Chaffee - Patricia C. Todd	64 62
1952	Shirley Fry - Doris Hart	A. Louise Brough - Maureen Connolly	108 64
1953	Shirley Fry - Doris Hart	A. Louise Brough - Margaret O. duPont	62 79 97
1954	Shirley Fry - Doris Hart	A. Louise Brough - Margaret O. duPont	64 64
1955	A. Louise Brough - Margaret O. duPont	Doris Hart - Shirley Fry	63 16 63
1956	A. Louise Brough - Margaret O. duPont	Betty R. Pratt - Shirley Fry	63 60
1957	A. Louise Brough - Margaret O. duPont	Althea Gibson - Darlene Hard	62 75
1958	Jeanne M. Arth - Darlene R. Hard	Althea Gibson - Maria Bueno	26 63 64
1959	Jeanne M. Arth - Darlene R. Hard	Maria Bueno - Sally Moore	62 63
1960	Maria Bueno - Darlene R. Hard	Ann Haydon - Deidre Catt	61 61
1961	Darlene R. Hard - Lesley Turner	Edda Buding - Yola Ramirez	64 57 60
1962	Darlene R. Hard - Maria Bueno	Karen H. Susman - Billie Jean Moffitt	46 63 62
1963	Robyn Ebbern - Margaret Smith	Darlene Hard - Maria Bueno	46 108 63
1964	Billie Jean Moffitt - Karen H. Susman	Margaret Smith - Lesley Turner	36 62 64
1965	Carole Caldwell Graebner - Nancy Richey	Billie Jean Moffitt - Karen H. Susman	64 64
1966	Maria Bueno - Nancy Richey	Billie Jean King - Rosemary Casals	63 64
1967	Rosemary Casals - Billie Jean King	Mary Ann Eisel - Donna F. Fales	46 63 64

Year	Champions	Runners-up	Score
1968	Maria Bueno - Margaret Smith Court	Billie Jean King - Rosemary Casals	46 97 86
1969	Francoise Durr - Darlene Hard	Margaret S. Court - Virginia Wade	06 64 64
1970	Margaret S. Court - Judy Tegart Dalton	Rosemary Casals - Virginia Wade	63 64
1971	Rosemary Casals - Judy Tegart Dalton	Gail Chanfreau - Francoise Durr	63 63
1972	Francoise Durr - Betty Stove	Margaret S. Court - Virginia Wade	63 16 63
1973	Margaret Smith Court - Virginia Wade	Billie Jean King - Rosemary Casals	36 63 75
1974	Rosemary Casals - Billie Jean King	Francoise Durr - Betty Stove	76 67 64
1975	Margaret Smith Court - Virginia Wade	Billie Jean King - Rosemary Casals	75 26 75
1976	Delina Boshoff - Ilana Kloss	Olga Morozova - Virginia Wade	61 64
1977	Martina Navratilova - Betty Stove	Renee Richards - Bettyann Stuart	61 76
1978	Billie Jean King - Martina Navratilova	Kerry M. Reid - Wendy Turnbull	76 64
1979	Betty Stove - Wendy Turnbull	Billie Jean King - Martina Navratilova	75 63
1980	Billie Jean King - Martina Navratilova	Pam Shriver - Betty Stove	76 75
1981	Anne Smith - Kathy Jordan	Rosemary Casals - Wendy Turnbull	63 63
1982	Rosemary Casals - Wendy Turnbull	Sharon Walsh - Barbara Potter	64 64
1983	Pam Shriver - Martina Navratilova	Rosalyn Fairbank - Candy Reynolds	67 61 63
1984	Pam Shriver - Martina Navratilova	Anne Hobbs - Wendy Turnbull	62 64
1985	Claudia Kohde-Kilsch - Helena Sukova	Martina Navratilova - Pam Shriver	67 62 63
1986	Pam Shriver - Martina Navratilova	Hana Mandlikova - Wendy Turnbull	64 36 63
1987	Pam Shriver - Martina Navratilova	Kathy Jordan - Elizabeth Smylie	57 64 62

National Mixed Doubles Finals, 1887–1987

Mixed Doubles has had a curious history as a national championship. It was originally played as part of the National Women's tournament hosted annually by the Philadelphia Cricket Club in St. Martin's, Pa. The first tournament was played in 1887, the year of the first national women's singles. That year, Virginia Stokes and Joseph S. Clark won the title. The 1888 tournament was won by Marion Wright and Joseph S. Clark who defeated Adelina Robinson — one of the great early women players — and Paul Johnson, 1-6, 6-5, 6-4, 6-3. Miss Wright and Clark repeated in 1889 and then were replaced by Mabel Cahill and Rodney Beach in 1890. In 1891, Miss Cahill won the title again, this time with M.R. Wright, defeating Grace Roosevelt and C.T. Lee in the final, 6-4, 6-0, 7-5.

However, those five early tournaments were not recognized as official by the U.S.N.L.T.A. which dated the record-keeping of the Mixed Doubles Championships from 1892. The winners in those finals follow:

Year	Champions	Runners-up	Score
1892	Mabel E. Cahill - Clarence Hobart	Elisabeth Moore - Rodney Beach	61 63
1893	Ellen C. Roosevelt - Clarence Hobart	Miss Bankson - Robert N. Willson, Jr	61 46 108 61
1894	Juliette P. Atkinson - Edwin P. Fischer	Mrs. McFadden - Gustav Remak, Jr.	63 62 61
1895	Juliette P. Atkinson - Edwin P. Fischer	Amy R. Williams - Mantle Fielding	46 86 62
1896	Juliette P. Atkinson - Edwin P. Fischer	Amy R. Williams - Mantle Fielding	62 63 63
1897	Laura Henson - D.L. Magruder	Maud Banks - R.A. Griffin	64 63 75
1898	Carrie B. Neely - Edwin P. Fischer	Helen Chapman - J.A. Hill	
1899	Elizabeth J. Rastall - Albert L. Hoskins	Jennie W. Craven - James P. Gardner	64 60 def.
1900	Margaret Hunnewell - Alfred Codman	T. Shaw - George Atkinson	119 63 61
1901	Marion Jones - Raymond D. Little	Myrtle McAteer - Dr. Clyde Stevens	64 64 75
1902	Elisabeth H. Moore - Wylie C. Grant	Elizabeth J. Rastall - Albert L. Hoskins	62 61
1903	Helen Chapman - Harry F. Allen	Carrie B. Neely - W.H. Rowland	64 75
1904	Elisabeth H. Moore - Wylie C. Grant	May Sutton - F.B. Dallas	62 61
1905	Mrs. Alice S. Hobart - Clarence Hobart	Elisabeth H. Moore - Edward B. Dewhurst	62 64
1906	Sarah Coffin - Edward B. Dewhurst	Margaret Johnson - J.B. Johnson	63 75
1907	May Sayres - Wallace F. Johnson	Natalie Wildey - H. Morris Tilden	61 75
1908	Edith E. Rotch - Nathaniel W. Niles	Louise Hammond - Raymond D. Little	64 46 64
1909	Hazel V. Hotchkiss - Wallace F. Johnson	Louise Hammond - Raymond D. Little	62 60
1910	Hazel V. Hotchkiss - Joseph R. Carpenter, Jr.	Edna Wildey - H. Morris Tilden	62 62
1911	Hazel V. Hotchkiss - Wallace F. Johnson	Edna Wildey - H. Morris Tilden	64 64
1912	Mary K. Browne - R.N. Williams, 2nd	Eleanora Sears - W.J. Clothier	64 26 119
1913	Mary K. Browne - Bill Tilden	Dorothy Green - C.S. Rogers	75 75
1914	Mary K. Browne - Bill Tilden	Margaretta Myers - J.R. Rowland	61 64
1915	Hazel H. Wightman - Harry C. Johnson	Molla Bjurstedt - Irving C. Wright	60 61
1916	Eleonora Sears - Willis F. Davis	Florence A. Ballin - Bill Tilden	64 75
1917	Molla Bjurstedt - Irving C. Wright	Florence A. Ballin - Bill Tilden	1012 61 63
1918	Hazel Hotchkiss Wightman - Irving C. Wright	Molla Bjurstedt - Fred Alexander	62 64
1919	Marion Zinderstein - Vincent Richards	Florence A. Ballin - Bill Tilden	26 119 62
1920	Hazel H. Wightman - Wallace F. Johnson	Molla B. Mallory - Craig Biddle	64 63

In 1921, the Mixed Doubles Championship was moved to the Longwood Cricket Club in Boston where it became part of the National Men's Doubles program which also included Father & Son Doubles and Senior Men's Doubles.

Year	Champions	Runners-up	Score
1921	Mary K. Browne - William Johnston	Molla B. Mallory - Bill Tilden	36 64 63
1922	Molla B. Mallory - Bill Tilden	Helen Wills - Howard Kinsey	64 63
1923	Molla B. Mallory - Bill Tilden	Kitty McKane - John B. Hawkes	63 26 108
1924	Helen N. Wills - Vincent Richards	Molla B. Mallory - Bill Tilden	68 75 60
1925	Kathleen McKane - John B. Hawkes	Ermintrude H. Harvey - Vincent Richards	62 64
1926	Elizabeth Ryan - Jean Borotra	Hazel H. Wightman - Rene LaCoste	64 75
1927	Eileen Bennett - Henri Cochet	Hazel H. Wightman - Rene LaCoste	62 60 63
1928	Helen N. Wills - John B. Hawkes	Edith Cross - Edgar F. Moon	61 63
1929	Betty Nuthall - George M. Lott, Jr.	Phyllis Covell - Henry W. Austin	63 63
1930	Edith Cross - Wilmer L. Allison	Marjore Morrill - Frank Shields	64 64
1931	Betty Nuthall - George M. Lott, Jr.	Anna McCune Harper - Wilmer Allison	63 63
1932	Sarah Palfrey - Frederick Perry	Helen Jacobs - Ellsworth Vines	63 75
1933	Elizabeth Ryan - H. Ellsworth Vines, Jr.	Sarah Palfrey - George W. Lott, Jr.	119 61
1934	Helen H. Jacobs - George M. Lott, Jr.	Elizabeth Ryan - Lester R. Stoefen	46 1311 62
1935	Sarah Palfrey Fabyan - Enrique Maier	Kay Stammers - Roderick Menzel	64 46 63
1936	Alice Marble - C.Gene Mako	Sarah Palfrey Fabyan - Donald Budge	63 62
1937	Sarah Palfrey Fabyan - Donald Budge	Sylvia Henrotin - Yvon Petra	62 810 60
1938	Alice Marble - J. Donald Budge	Thelma Coyne - John Bromwich	61 62
1939	Alice Marble - Harry C. Hopman	Sarah Palfrey Fabyan - Elwood Cooke	97 61
1940	Alice Marble - Robert L. Riggs	Dorothy Bundy - Jack Kramer	97 61
1941	Sarah Palfrey Cooke - John A. Kramer	Pauline Betz - Bobby Riggs	46 64 64
1942	A. Louise Brough - Frederick Schroeder, Jr.	Patricia C. Todd - Alejo Russell	36 61 64
1943	Margaret Osborne - William F. Talbert	Pauline Betz - Pancho Segura	108 64
1944	Margaret Osborne - William F. Talbert	Dorothy Bundy - Lt. W. Donald McNeill	62 63
1945	Margaret Osborne - William F. Talbert	Doris Hart - Bob Falkenberg	64 64
1946	Margaret Osborne - William F. Talbert	A. Louise Brough - Robert Kimbrell	63 64
1947	A. Louise Brough - John Bromwich	Gussie Moran - Pancho Segura	63 61
1948	A. Louise Brough - Thomas P. Brown, Jr.	Margaret O. duPont - Bill Talbert	64 64
1949	A. Louise Brough - Eric Sturgess	Margaret O. duPont - Bill Talbert	46 63 75
1950	Margaret O. duPont - Kenneth McGregor	Doris Hart - Frank Sedgman	64 36 63
1951	Doris Hart - Frank Sedgman	Shirley Fry - Mervyn Rose	63 62
1952	Doris Hart - Frank Sedgman	Thelma C. Long - Lew Hoad	63 75
1953	Doris Hart - E. Victor Seixas, Jr.	Julia Ann Sampson - Rex Hartwig	62 46 64
1954	Doris Hart - E. Victor Seixas, Jr.	Margaret O. duPont - Ken Rosewall	46 61 61
1955	Doris Hart - E. Victor Seixas, Jr.	Shirley Fry - Lew Hoad	97 61
1956	Margaret Osborne duPont - Kenneth Rosewall	Darlene Hard - Lew Hoad	97 61
1957	Althea Gibson - Kurt Neilsen	Darlene Hard - Bob Howe	63 97
1958	Margaret Osborne duPont - Neale Fraser	Maria Bueno - Alex Olmedo	63 36 97
1959	Margaret Osborne duPont - Neale Fraser	Janet Hopps - Bob Mark	75 1315 62
1960	Margaret Osborne duPont - Neale Fraser	Maria Bueno - Antonio Palafox	63 62
1961	Margaret Smith - Robert Mark	Darlene Hard - Dennis Ralston	def.
1962	Margaret Smith - Fred Stolle	Lesley Turner - Frank Froehling III	75 62
1963	Margaret Smith - Ken Fletcher	Judy Tegart - Ed Rubinoff	36 86 62
1964	Margaret Smith - John Newcombe	Judy Tegart - Ed Rubinoff	108 46 63
1965	Margaret Smith - Fred Stolle	Judy Tegart - Frank Froehling III	62 62
1966	Donna Floyd Fales - Owen Davidson	Carol H. Aucamp - Ed Rubinoff	61 63
1967	Billie Jean King - Owen Davidson	Rosemary Casals - Stan Smith	63 62

Open Champions— Mixed Doubles

Year	Champions	Runners-up	Score
1968	Not held		
1969	Margaret S. Court - Martin Riessen	Francoise Durr - Dennis Ralston	75 63
1970	Margaret S. Court - Martin Riessen	Judy T. Dalton - Frew McMillan	64 64
1971	Billie Jean King - Owen Davidson	Betty Stove - Rob Maud	63 75
1972	Margaret S. Court - Martin Riessen	Rosemary Casals - Ilie Nastase	63 75
1973	Billie Jean King - Owen Davidson	Margaret S. Court - Marty Riessen	63 36 76
1974	Pam Teeguarden - Geoff Masters	Chris Evert - Jimmy Connors	61 76
1975	Rosemary Casals - Richard Stockton	Billie Jean King - Fred Stolle	63 76
1976	Billie Jean King - Phil Dent	Betty Stove - Frew McMillan	36 62 75
1977	Betty Stove - Frew McMillan	Billie Jean King - Vitas Gerulaitis	62 36 63
1978	Betty Stove - Frew McMillan	Billie Jean King - Ray Ruffels	63 76
1979	Greer Stevens - Bob Hewitt	Betty Stove - Frew McMillan	63 75
1980	Wendy Turnbull - Martin Riessen	Betty Stove - Frew McMillan	75 62
1981	Anne Smith - Kevin Curren	JoAnne Russell - Steve Denton	64 76
1982	Anne Smith - Kevin Curren	Barbara Potter - Ferdi Taygan	67 76 76
1983	Elizabeth Sayers - John Fitzgerald	Barbara Potter - Ferdi Taygan	36 63 64
1984	Manuela Maleeva - Tom Gullikson	Elizabeth Sayers - John Fitzgerald	26 75 64
1985	Martina Navratilova - Heinz Gunthardt	Elizabeth Smylie - John Fitzgerald	63 64
1986	Raffaella Reggi - Sergio Casal	Martina Navratilova - Peter Fleming	64 64
1987	Martina Navratilova - Emilio Sanchez	Betsy Nagelsen - Paul Annacone	64 67 76

171

The National Championships: 1881–1987

Although the five major championships — men's and women's singles, men's and women's doubles and mixed doubles — have been played together as part of the U.S. Open program in recent years, such was not the case during much of the history of these championships.

Men's doubles, for instance, are now being contested at their eighth site since 1881 and have used three of those sites twice for a series of years. Of the premier championships, women's singles have suffered the least dislocation, having been contested in only three locales since 1887.

Doubles, particularly, have undergone extensive changes in format over the years. Most often, they have been a play-through tournament as is now the case with all events. However, for many years, the men's doubles final was a challenge round in which the defending champions played one match against the survivor of the national tournament. The men's doubles format at one time called for a single-match championship between Eastern and Western winners or for a round-robin of sorts among a variety of sectional winners at various times during their history.

Here are the sites for the championships in all events since 1881:

Men's Singles

1881 – 1914	The Casino, Newport, R.I.
1915 – 20	West Side Tennis Club, N.Y.
1921 – 23	Germantown Cricket Club, Philadelphia
1924 – 77	West Side Tennis Club
1978 –	USTA National Tennis Center

Men's Doubles

1881 – 86	The Casino, Newport
1887	Orange Tennis Club, Mountain Station, N.J.
1888 – 89	Staten Island Cricket Club, N.Y.
1890 – 92	The Casino, Newport
1893	St. George Cricket Club, Chicago
1894 – 1914	The Casino, Newport
1915 – 16	West Side Tennis Club
1917 – 33	Longwood Cricket Club
1934	Germantown Cricket Club
1935 – 41	Longwood Cricket Club
1942 – 45	West Side Tennis Club
1946 – 67	Longwood Cricket Club
1968 – 77	West Side Tennis Club
1978 –	USTA National Tennis Center

Women's Singles

1887 – 1920	Philadelphia Cricket Club
1921 – 77	West Side Tennis Club
1978 –	USTA National Tennis Center

Women's Doubles

1887 – 1920	Philadelphia Cricket Club
1921 – 33	West Side Tennis Club
1934	Germantown Cricket Club
1935 – 41	Longwood Cricket Club, Boston
1942 – 45	West Side Tennis Club
1946 – 67	Longwood Cricket Club
1968 – 77	West Side Tennis Club
1978 –	USTA National Tennis Center

Mixed Doubles

1892 – 1920	Philadelphia Cricket Club
1921 – 34	West Side Tennis Club
1935 – 41	Longwood Cricket Club
1942 – 67	West Side Tennis Club
1969 – 77	West Side Tennis Club
1978 –	USTA National Tennis Center

While nine sites have been employed for the national championship events in the past 107 years, the West Side Tennis Club in Forest Hills, Queens, New York City, has hosted 209 of the total of 509 championship events. Totals for other venues are: Philadelphia Cricket Club 95 championships, Longwood 82, The Casino 64, USTA National Tennis Center 50, Germantown 5, Staten Island 2, and Orange Tennis Club and St. George's C.C. one each.

172

Tom Leonard
Cliff Letcher
John Letts
Jonny Levine
Chris Lewis
Mark Lewis
Carl Limberger
Scott Lipton
David Livingston
John Lloyd
William Lloyd
Jose Lopez-Maeso
Jorge Lozano
John Lucas
Andy Luccesi
Peter Lundgren
Bob Lutz

Kate Latham
Andrea Leand
Duk Hee Lee
Zenda Leiss
Susan Leo
Trey Lewis
Catarina Lindqvist
Maria Lindstrom
Elizabeth Little
Stephanie London
Marcie Louie
Peanut Louie
Gail Lovera
Heather Ludloff

M

Geoff MacDonald
Mike Machette
Francisco Maciel
David MacPherson
Ali Madani
Gene Malin
Ola Malmqvist
Amos Mansdorf
Jacques Manset
Bruce Manson
Mike Margolin
John Marks
Billy Martin
Geoff Martinez
Mario Martinez
Wally Masur
Luiz Mattar
John Mattke
Richard Matuszewski
Alex Mayer
Gene Mayer
Fernando Maynetto
Chris Mayotte
Tim Mayotte

Bill Maze
Scott McCain
John McCurdy
John McEnroe
Patrick McEnroe
Jim McManus
Frew McMillan
Peter McNamara
Paul McNamee
Fred McNair
Miloslav Mecir
Steve Meister
Sashi Menon
Rick Meyer
Claudio Mezzadri
Glenn Michibata
Allen Miller
Craig Miller
Matt Mitchell
Bernie Mitton
Tony Mmoh
Barry Moir
Kevin Moir
Jon Molin
Ivan Molina
Terry Moor
Ray Moore
Augustin Moreno
Gilles Moretton
Michael Mortensen
Cassio Motta
Buster Mottram
Gary Muller
Antonio Munoz
Pender Murphy
David Mustard
Thomas Muster
Mike Myburg

Cammy MacGregor
Cynthia MacGregor
Ivanna Madruga-Osses
Katerina Maleeva
Manuela Maleeva
Hana Mandlikova
Helena Manset
Cricket Manuel
Sue Mappin
Stacy Margoli
Regina Marsikova
Jan Martin
Susan Mascarin
Kathy May
Roberta McCallum
Shannon McCarthy
Sheila McInerney
Lori McNeil
Patricia Medrado
Silke Meier

Marcella Mesker
Carrie Meyer
Florenza Mihai
Anne Minter
Elizabeth Minter
Tina Mochizuki
Claudia Montiero
Karen Moos
Diane Morrison
Lindsay Morse
Gabriela Mosca
Alycia Moulton
Jennifer Mundel
Patrizia Murgo

N

Jaro Navratil
Ilie Nastase
Billy Nealon
Todd Nelson
John Newcombe
Bruce Nichols
Randy Nixon
Yannick Noah
Jan Norback
Karel Novacek
Juan Nunez
Joakim Nystrom

Hu Na
Jean Nachand
Betsy Nagelsen
Martina Navratilova
Vicki Nelson
Janet Newberry
Betty Newfield
Chris Newton
Nancy Neviaser
Beth Norton
Mary Norwood

O

Gianni Ocleppo
Nduka Odizor
Tom Okker
Manuel Orantes
Bruno Oresar
Guillermo Oropez
Jim Osborne
Ricki Osterthun
Marco Ostoja
Charlie Owens

Cathy O'Brien
Germaine Ohaco
Emiko Okagawa
Kumiko Okamoto

Christine O'Neil
Wendy Overton

P

John Paish
Leo Palin
Doug Palm
Adriano Panatta
Claudio Panatta
Ben Papell
Al Parker
Onny Parun
Charlie Pasarell
Ray Pascale
Wayne Pascoe
David Pate
Andrew Pattison
Tim Pawsat
Brad Pearce
Victor Pecci
Diego Perez
Shahar Perkiss
Mikael Pernfors
Glenn Petrovic
Hank Pfister
Libor Pimek
Brent Pirow
Claudio Pistolesi
Pascal Portes
Jerome Potier
Belus Prajoux
Gianluci Pozzi
Willem Prinsloo
Jim Pugh
Mel Purcell

Marietta Pakker
Pascale Paradis
Claudia Pasquale
Mercedes Paz
Michaela Pazderova
Helene Pelletier
Carmen Perea
Mariana Perez-Roldan
Brenda Perry
Eva Pfaff
Tery Phelps
Mary Lou Piatek
Marie Pinterova
Joyce Portman
Claudia Porwik
Daniela Porzio
Barbara Potter
Kerryn Pratt
Jane Preyer
Nicole Provis
Wiltrud Probst

Ginny Purdy

Q

Maeve Quinlan

R

Olli Rahnasto
Dennis Ralston
Raul Ramirez
Pedro Rebolledo
Walter Redondo
Horace Reid
Raz Reid
Richey Reneberg
Peter Rennert
Keith Richardson
Cliff Richey
Karl Richter
Marty Riessen
Joey Rive
Michael Robertson
Terry Rocavert
Christophe Roger-Vasseli
John Ross
Derrick Rostagno
Brad Rowe
Rick Rudeen
Ray Ruffels

Emilse Raponi-Longo
Felicia Raschiatore
Marita Redondo
Raffaella Reggi
Stephanie Rehe
Kerry Reid
Elna Reinach
Monica Reinach
Ronni Reis
Brenda Remilton
Candy Reynolds
Renee Richards
Julie Richardson
Nancy Richey
Iris Riedel
Susan Rimes
Kathy Rinaldi
Debbie Robb
Susan Rollinson
Lucia Romanov
Barbara Rossi
Eleni Rossides
Kym Ruddell
Gretchen Rush
JoAnne Russell
Susan Russo
Virginia Ruzici

S

Roberto Saad
Christian Saceanu
John Sadri
Dan Saltz
Emilio Sanchez
Javier Sanchez
Howard Sands
Fred Sauer
Nick Saviano
Bill Scanlon
Michiel Schapers
David Schneider
Howard Schoenfield
Hans Schwaier
Bud Schultz
Larry Scott
Butch Seewagen

Derek Segal
Florin Segarceanu
Robert Seguso
Pat Serret
Dave Sherbeck
Eric Sherbeck
Leif Shiras
Mike Shore
Tim Siegel
David Siegler
Hans Simonsson
Stefan Simonsson
Jeff Simpson
Russell Simpson
Jasjit Singh
Beejong Sisson
Horst Skoff
Pavel Slozil
Tomas Smid
Bill Smith
Jonathan Smith
Stan Smith
Roger Smith
Joao Soares
Harold Solomon
Milan Srejber
Ronald Stadler
Larry Stefanki
Ulf Stenlund
Sherwood Stewart
Christo Steyn
Dick Stockton
Fred Stolle
Charles Strode
Morris Strode
Henrik Sundstrom
Jonas B. Svensson
Chris Sylvan
Andrew Sznajder